UNCHAINED

A Man's Journey from Abuse to
Healing to Saving Lives

RON POST

ISBN 979-8-9874740-0-6(paperback)
       979-8-9874740-1-3(ebook)

For security reasons, some names were changed.

The author's website offers free devotions and means to contact the author: www.ronpost.org.

To visit the ongoing ministries founded by the author, please visit Medical Team International at www.medicalteams.org and Mission Increase at www.missionincrease.org.

With gratitude to the following team members of Christian Editing and Design, www.christianeditinganddesign.com:

Jen Miller, Developmental Editor
Karen Weigand, Line Editor
Bethany Clark, Proofreader
Sandy Armstrong, Cover Designer
Shannon Herring, Interior Designer

Printed in the United States of America.

∽ℭ∼

To Jean Post—my beloved partner in life, my wife since 1959, mother of our children Bill, Sheri, and Dawn, and grandmother of six.

Jean and I were opposites in personalities. I'm the charge ahead, get it done right now kind of person, and Jean loved to take time to think about a circumstance before moving forward. She listened, prayed, encouraged, and supported this Type A personality.

When God called me to begin Medical Teams, Jean was by my side, urging me on, wanting to help in any way she could. She played a vital role in founding the ministry. Without her, Medical Teams would have been more challenging financially. Jean organized and established twenty-one fundraising banquets every year for ten years to introduce new partners to our mission. The work she did was priceless.

Jean was a great mother to our children, always there for them and praying. She was the anchor and cheerleader of our family. She loved our children and grandchildren deeply.

My beloved Jean spent an extended period of time in memory care before she went to be with the Lord on December 5, 2022, just as this book was about to go to press. What she accomplished will live on forever in the hearts of many.

One of Jean's favorite Bible passages was Psalm 119:11: "I have hidden your word in my heart that I might not sin against you." She loved reading the Bible. For ten years, she attended Bible Study Fellowship, one of the most in-depth studies (if not the most) outside of seminary.

She hid God's Word in her heart, and those living words became the very fiber of her being. I read Scripture to Jean after her illness progressed, and I was amazed at how she finished some of the verses before I completed reading them. She inspired us to spend more time in the Bible.

My love for Jean has no end. Nothing can separate us, not even death.

Thank you, my beloved.

CONTENTS

INTRODUCTION

S tanding behind the stage, soon to face thirteen thousand people, I felt nervous and unworthy. I wondered how someone like me could be the recipient of Kiwanis International's highest honor—the World Service Medal. The notion felt surreal as I waited anxiously to be called from the shadows and presented with the medal.

Such an honor. If they knew my past, would I be standing here? Visions of my early broken life reeled through my mind. *How had someone like me overcome such brokenness to now stand here?* Other humbling and amazing honors shifted into focus as my hands sweated and my heart pounded. *With such odds against me, how had I begun two service ministries that are now helping millions of people worldwide?* I felt like an imposter. *With only a high school diploma, how had someone like me been awarded two honorary doctorates?* I stood in awe and disbelief, waiting with my wife, Jean, who had always been my greatest encourager.

Unchained demonstrates what one ordinary individual can accomplish against the odds, motivating others to find and use their innate gifts for a greater purpose. This book is my true story that, like many, began with the conflict, pain, and brokenness of childhood abuse. But a stunning turn of events in my healing journey catapulted me into an incredible uncharted worldwide pilgrimage of unimaginable circumstances. My heart and life were transformed into a deep well of meaning and purpose.

I could not entirely tell this story without including Jean. She also made peace with her troubled childhood and gained wonderful experiences serving others. I could not fully share my extraordinary journey without including key stories from the book I authored in 1999, *Created for Purpose*, now out of print. Much of what I share is the journey of establishing Medical Teams International and walking unchained from my past to serve with the volunteer teams in horrendous and miraculous circumstances around the world.

Unchained may alternately bring you tears of heartbreak and moments of laughter. If you're struggling to overcome challenges, I believe you'll gain a heightened desire to find inner healing, purpose, and fulfillment. If you're seeking or already enjoying the rewards of living a healed and purposed life, I believe my story will further affirm and equip you to overcome future obstacles.

Life is a series of threads, good and bad, woven together in our lives to grow, strengthen, and shape us to live our best lives while helping others discover their God-given gifts and purpose. The results are stunning, as you'll see from my transformative journey.

Thank you for joining me. Welcome to my journey.

CHAPTER ONE

WALKING INTO DARKNESS

You were once darkness, but now you are light in the Lord.

— Ephesians 5:8

B arbed wire surrounded the crowded seven-acre compound, and armed guards were ready to shoot any of the forty thousand refugees who dared try to escape. I was familiar with the compound's size because I'd grown up on a seven-acre tract. The glaring difference was my childhood in the tract was enjoyed in the security and plenty of the U.S. and the comforts of San Bernardino, California. I was stunned that the refugee camp was an entire city of people crammed into a tiny rural space.

The unfortunate forty thousand were trying to survive on a daily ration of two spoonfuls of rice. Lack of nutrition made the people more susceptible to illnesses and diseases. They had absolutely nothing—no homeland, homes, possessions . . . and no hope. They had escaped the vicious dictator of their country, Cambodia, only to face starvation, sickness, and early death across the border in Thailand. It was November 1979.

Between 1975 and 1979, thousands of Cambodians fled their homes in terror of their cruel prime minister, Pol Pot. Those were the days of the "killing fields," a term popularized by the movie of the same name.

The death toll was about three million. The desperate people were hungry, sick, and grieving the many loved ones who had perished, those who were near death, and the loss of their now-forsaken homes and homeland. Weak with suffering, they had stumbled across the border for safety as if seeking a quiet place to die in hopelessness.

My team and I had learned of the conditions before arriving, but nothing could have prepared us for the reality. The camp gate swung open, and our first volunteer medical team entered the sea of needy and dying people wearing black clothing that hung loosely on their thin, frail frames. The sight was heartbreaking, and the stench of human waste from open trenches was so overpowering I had to restrain the impulse to cover my nose to keep from vomiting. I struggled with both while keenly aware that the refugees' suffering was staggering, so much greater than any pain I had ever experienced. We grieved the terrible cost the refugees bore.

I searched the faces as we moved toward the hospital ward. The migrants' eyes were as empty and dark as their clothing. They appeared to be staring at nothingness. The expansive needs presented a mission I had not before encountered, nor had my volunteer team of physicians, nurses, and medics.

Questions raced through my mind. *Is this where we're supposed to be? Will the team be up to the complex tasks of treating diseases they've never seen? What are the volunteers thinking and feeling?* We were Americans, and mass tragedies of this proportion didn't happen in our homeland.

World Vision International had assigned our medical team to the vast hospital. The thatched roof served as a canopy over gravel floors. Rows of cots stretched more than three hundred feet. The space could accommodate caring for hundreds of outpatients and 125 inpatients.

As we strode through the maze of cots toward our assigned stations, each face we encountered reflected more pain and anguish than I had seen up to that time in my life. The air was rife with distressful moaning. A young woman cried out in pain. Her infant lay near death beside her, the baby's delicate skin threatened by protruding bones. The unmistakable signs of starvation confronted my comfortable life in America.

Pleading eyes of the desperately ill followed our every move, hoping for relief. A fifteen-year-old boy groaned from a gunshot wound to his abdomen. The bullet had exited just above his rectum, causing a continual seepage of feces.

Questions That Pummeled Me

Who am I that I should live in America rather than experience this devastation, grief, hardship, and suffering? Why am I so blessed?

I considered how God creates every human with the same basic needs and desires—to care for our families, enjoy life, and stay healthy. I wrestled with the fact that thousands of people have been stripped of those abilities. They struggle to survive physically while their hearts tear with each sight and sound of family members and friends suffering and dying around them.

The disparity between a nearby sick man and me was only our birthplaces. Had I been born in Cambodia, I might have been one lying in the makeshift hospital, suffering and praying for help or the relief of death.

> How often had I taken America and my daily blessings for granted?

I had somehow supposed that American citizenship was an earned right and that we were superior people, blessed because of our right choices. *How have I ignored oppressed and hurting people for so long?*

3

I had much to learn and many changes I needed to make in my life.

The suffering around me was too terrible for words—human wailing, groaning, emaciated bodies fighting disease, the air saturated with stench.

How can I possibly make a difference here? I'm just an ordinary man, a businessperson without preparation for this role among such atrocities.

I retraced the events that had brought me halfway around the globe, carrying a resounding question. *Why was I given this monumental assignment?* The answer hadn't come from days of fasting on a mountaintop or kneeling at a church altar. My calling to Cambodia had come while sitting in my easy chair in the comfort of my U.S. home.

Like others called to serve, I felt unequal to the calling. I felt overcome, inadequate, and out of place. I realized I felt how God intended so I would look to Him, not myself, for answers and solutions. I was not in that horrid scenario by accident but as part of God's masterful plan to further shape me by compassion for those in dire suffering, to teach me to hear and follow His voice, and to better equip me to love and serve those in need.

CHAPTER TWO

GOD'S PLAN

"I know that you can do all things; no
purpose of yours can be thwarted."

— Job 42:2

Before that Thailand trip, Jean and I had sat together in
the comfort of our home in Salem, Oregon, watching the
evening news. The broadcast showed devastating scenes of
desperate Cambodian refugees. I had no idea on that cool, rainy
evening in 1979 that I would soon be in Thailand, confronted with
the horrible stench of sickness and death.

Moved by the unforgettable images on the screen, Jean and I
looked at each other, wishing there was something we could do
to help. We were horrified at the sight of what appeared to be the
emaciated body of a teenage girl, starved to death, being retrieved
from a rice field by aid workers. My gaze quickly shifted to our
healthy, beautiful teenage daughter, Sheri, sleeping sweetly on our
couch, and a sudden piercing thought struck me: *That ravaged girl
in Thailand, limp with death, could have been our precious Sheri had
we been born Cambodian.*

The hopes and dreams of the deceased teen had been cut short,
denied by an early, tragic death. Again, questions and facts warred
in me. *Why were we blessed to be born in the U.S. instead of Cambodia?*

We didn't choose to be born here, and the parents of the Cambodian teen hadn't chosen to be born there!

As I sat immersed in such thoughts, I was startled by a sudden mental vision and inner voice:

Recruit a medical team and lead them to the refugee camp to aid the desperately needy refugees — two weeks from now.

What?

The simple and precise plan was crystal clear in my mind, as though someone had sketched it on paper and handed it to me.

Absently shaking my head, I grasped the enormity of such an undertaking. *No one could manage such a colossal feat in such a brief time!* I was a veteran businessperson and familiar with organizational processes, so I knew such a plan would take months to materialize: recruiting a medical team, gathering funding, and everything else needed would have to fall into place, which wasn't common. Any organizational endeavor, especially one of this magnitude, was typically fraught with setbacks and other challenges.

How can I possibly persuade the medical community to join this plan—and be ready to go in two weeks? Why would medical professionals follow me? I have no medical background; I'm a businessman. Even if I could persuade medical professionals, how would I get them to Thailand in only two weeks?

What about supplies and the funds needed for shipping? I don't know anything about medical needs.

The questions were an unruly crowd in me, shouting, *Impossible!*

Afraid to share the plan with Jean, I balked. But I felt so deeply motivated that I couldn't keep the plan to myself for long. I blurted out, "We need to organize a medical team and go to Thailand. Right away."

Jean's response floored me. An emphatic "Yes!" She added, "I didn't want to say anything, but I knew we had to help those people." What an affirmation and tide of encouragement!

Her agreement increased my ability to see the plan through the eyes of faith. There was no turning back. The refugees were in desperate need of medical care, and the call in us was clearly from God. From that moment, we brainstormed how to put the pieces of His plan into action.

We first needed more information about the refugees' medical needs.

God's Call to All

Jean and I supported two missionary friends, Marty and Jan Larson, serving in Bangkok, Thailand, through the mission New Tribes. We believed the Larsons would know if the medical needs were urgent—though God's two-week timing had implied the urgency.

I immediately called. Neither Marty nor Jan was available, but I spoke with the director. He confirmed the refugees' plight was urgent and many were dying from lack of timely medical care.

My heart hurt deeply for the people, and I felt affirmed by the director's urgency that God had indeed called Jean and me to this mission.

I then called the KEZI-TV news reporter Don Clark, who had broadcasted the story we'd watched earlier that evening. It was now midnight, and his response wasn't enthusiastic. "Do you know how many weird calls we get?" he asked rhetorically . . . but listened. He would later share his initial thoughts about my impromptu call. "Here's a man, calling at midnight telling me he wants to take a medical team to the Cambodians! But I listened. He was sincere, and there was something special about that call. I said, 'Mr. Post, I don't know what I can do, but whatever you do, I'll cover the story.'" Don would become the first newsperson to cover our team's work in Thailand.

He suggested I call Mike Donahue at KOIN-TV in Portland and Senator Mark Hatfield, believing they were better informed of the needs.

Compassionate individuals in the media—television, radio, and news-papers—would be among God's key people for a successful mission. Reporters and camera crews came forward, wanting to be involved in what would become, to our awe, a significant movement of God. Even today as I recall that time, I'm astounded by God's power and divinity. Over the coming years, reporters would accompany our teams and professionally cover the stories. Behind the scenes, heartbroken, they would weep with us over the horrifying conditions we all witnessed.

The following morning, I called Senator Hatfield's office in Washington, D.C. He was unavailable. I hoped to learn more about the refugees' needs quickly, so I spoke with one of his assistants and explained the relief plan. He shared that the senator's attention was on the situation and confirmed that the medical needs were urgent. He assured me that someone would call me.

I was stunned when a call came from World Vision's president's sec-retary. She said they'd received a request to recruit a medical team for a field hospital ward in the Thailand refugee camp. At that time in World Vision's growth (1979), they had not before recruited medi-cal teams. God appeared to be calling those willing to serve rather than those with prior experience meeting such enormous needs. I was startled when she asked, "Mr. Post, can you recruit medical teams?" Another confirmation of God's directive in me.

Without a thought, I answered, "Yes!"

"Good!" she said. "We'll send a representative to Portland to meet with you."

I was astonished by what I'd seen God do within a mere twenty-four hours, yet familiar feelings of inadequacy welled inside me. After all, World Vision was an enormous international relief agency! *Surely, they have more and better means than me to recruit medical teams!*

Despite seeing God's work through the immediate connections I'd made, I felt more pressure to accomplish the impossible. *Why did I say yes so quickly to World Vision? Why me, Lord? I have no international experience. And what about all the unanswered questions?* World Vision counting on me, an ordinary businessman, was hard to believe. *Lord, I know You gave me this plan, but now what?*

Realizing my involvement was past the point of return, I relinquished my concerns to God with a sigh. Instantly, I felt strength, as if my spirit were squaring its shoulders and urging me to trust God, work hard, and see what would happen.

By Faith

A pastor friend suggested I seek the advice of two former missionary doctors in Portland. He gave me their names, and I telephoned them and explained the mission vision. They agreed to meet me at a Portland restaurant at noon the next day! For support, I asked Jean and my physician, Dr. Earl Van Volkinburg, to accompany me.

Then I called Mike Donahue at KOIN-TV, who would become a dear friend. I was surprised to be put directly through to Mike. He listened intently to my story and responded, "Ron, why don't you let all the television and radio stations and newspapers know about your meeting tomorrow?"

Unfamiliar with press conference protocol, I followed his suggestion but expected no one from the media to show. That doubt eliminated my anxiety, and I was eager about the next morning's meeting.

I left early for the hour's drive. Jean and Dr. Van Volkinburg would drive together a bit later, and a World Vision representative planned to join us.

An hour later, walking into the restaurant, the two Portland doctors confronted me, very agitated. "What's going on here?"

"What do you mean?" I was surprised and concerned, not knowing why they were upset.

"That room is full of reporters!" My stomach tightened as I listened. "We believed this was supposed to be an informational meeting with *you*," he added. "We didn't know you were bringing reporters!"

My anxiety catapulted, and I realized I should have informed the doctors of the impromptu press invitations. I felt terrible about my oversight and apologized. As they followed me to the room, unappeased, my thoughts were in prayer. *Lord, help me get through this.*

Upon entering, we were blinded by the lights of television cameras. My heart raced as panic seized me. Fortunately, my sensibilities as a seasoned businessman kicked in, and I calmly invited everyone to be seated.

I took a seat at the end of the long table, and when Jean and Dr. Van Volkinburg arrived, they quietly eased into the vacant seats at the opposite end, near the door. I longed to sit beside them for nearer moral support and the beckoning door!

I broke the ice by initiating a conversation about the situation in the Cambodian refugee camps in Thailand. The interaction was polite, cameras rolling, but the doctors' angry faces reminded me I was in hostile territory. One interjected, "Please share your plan."

I relayed the plan: recruit a medical team and take the team to Thailand in two weeks. Waiting for responses felt like an eternity.

The other doctor responded. "You can't expect a team to be ready in two weeks. It takes months to put something like this together."

The first doctor agreed. "You can't expect doctors to leave their practices and nurses to get time off that soon. This will take months." I wanted to crawl under the table.

The group was subdued, awaiting my response. Familiar doubts assailed me. *Are the doctors right? Why is this initiative going wrong if the call was from God?*

The plan did seem impossible. Still, I felt strongly about moving forward with the plan God had shown me, though the unanswered questions felt like phantoms refusing to leave an old haunt. *How am I going to get people to volunteer—this week? What about the supplies we'll need? Where will I get the finances?*

Thoughts of the apostle Peter intruded. Without forethought, he had stepped out of a boat in a raging storm and walked to Jesus on water. It wasn't until he realized what he was doing that he began to sink into fear and doubt.

In blind faith, I had stepped onto the surface of deep water and taken steps, following God. Now I was sinking, and like Peter, I cried out to God. *Lord, I believe You called me to this seemingly impossible mission, but I need the ways and means. Please, Lord, help me!*

Dr. Van Volkinburg broke the silence with a reversed scenario. "Ron, if someone called you with such a plan, what's the first thing you'd ask?"

"How soon can you go?" I hadn't hesitated. I laughed nervously and felt the room's tension ease a bit.

Dr. Van Volkinburg smiled and offered, "I could go in two weeks."

"Earl, are you volunteering?" I asked, hope rising.

"Yes!" His answer was emphatic.

With an infusion of renewed hope, I enthusiastically confirmed. "Great! You're my first volunteer!"

Suddenly, the wall of impossibilities vanished. Dr. Van Volkinburg's response was the pivotal turn toward quickly assembling a medical team. A veil had lifted, everyone appearing to see the plan through God's eyes and considering that "with God all things are possible" (Matthew 19:26).

In an instant, the mood had changed, and the doctors agreed the plan could work. We adjourned with everyone smiling. Despite the shark-attacking doubts, God's plan was still afloat.

Reporters fired questions at me. Unlike when I had made my shaky entrance, my confidence was once again rooted in the fact that the plan was not my invention but God's. The mission's fate was in His hands. I simply needed to keep walking forward, my eyes on Jesus with faith in His great power.

A reporter asked, "Do you really believe you can assemble a team and be in Thailand in two weeks?"

"Do you believe in God?" I asked.

"Yes," she answered without faltering.

I nodded. "I do too, and if God wants us to be there in two weeks, we will be!" She included that quote in her news story.

God was teaching me and others an essential mindset:

Hold tight to what you believe in your heart. Stand firm!

I better understood that God was in control of whatever would happen. My job was to be available and to pray that others would hear God's call and follow.

I soon discovered I was just one small part of God's grand design. The Cambodian refugees were waiting.

> "Ask the Lord of the harvest, therefore, to send out workers into his harvest field."
> — Matthew 9:38

Human Impossibilities Are God's Realities

Before I left the meeting, a television reporter said, "Ron, if you give us a telephone number before tonight's broadcast, we'll be happy to display it so people will know where to respond. I'm sure the other stations will do the same."

My thoughts paced. My home phone was only one line and not a Portland number. *Will people call long-distance?* (This was long before cell phones.) *Ideally, we need a toll-free line.* I considered the few hours remaining before the 6:00 p.m. telecast. The current time was 1:30 p.m. I had an hour's drive home and only four and a half hours to acquire a toll-free number.

I rushed back to Salem and called Reg Farnsworth, a friend who had converted a Market Street house into an office. He quickly agreed to let us use a room.

A friend from church worked with the phone company, so I called him and asked if the company would be willing to donate a toll-free line. "Yes, I think so," he said, "but it'll take about two weeks."

"Two weeks?" I said, incredulous.

"Well, how soon do you need them, Ron?"

"By tonight!" Panic and doubt again taunted me.

Surprise and helplessness were evident in his reply. "What? I can't do that!"

I pleaded, "I need the lines before 6:00 p.m. *tonight*. Will you see what you can do?"

An hour later, he called and said triumphantly, "You got it!" Relief and awe flooded me.

He relayed the toll-free number, and I called all the news outlets—television, radio, and newspapers.

The rapidly developing mission had received the donation of an office and toll-free line within two hours of my return home—two impossible feats from a human standpoint. Everything needed for the plan's kickoff was divinely falling into place. With each step, God patiently reminded me that He was the leader, working everything out, and I was the follower, doing whatever He asked. Moses came to mind. He had gone to Pharaoh by God's directive and asked him to free the Israelites from slavery. An impossible request for Moses, a mere man. But he was also the instrument God had chosen, and God is the One who makes the impossible a reality.

In the past, for any task I needed, I'd either complete it myself or pay someone. I was unaccustomed to asking for volunteers and donations. Now I was dependent on volunteer help from others. The experience clarified for me the apostle Paul's description of the body of Christ—all members working together, using their appointed skills while depending on others to do the same. The mission God had called me to pioneer with other volunteers was not ours; it was God's. We had agreed to be part of His plan and were moving forward in faith.

By 5:30 p.m., Jean and I had set up a long table in the loaned office and were waiting for the six o'clock newscast. Two borrowed telephones and our home television stared back at us. As the clock ticked slowly toward 6:00 p.m., my palms sweated, and I wrestled with more questions and doubts. *Will the media even air the story? Will anyone call? Are there other people who feel the chains of the Cambodian refugees and share our sense of helplessness?*

When the news came on, my heart raced. Only minutes into the broadcast, a reporter said, "A Salem man is trying to assemble a volunteer medical team to travel to the Cambodian refugee camps in Thailand. Here is the number to call for information."

Seconds after the toll-free number appeared on the screen, the two phones rang. Jean and I looked at each other in surprise and sprang to work.

A voice through my receiver said, "Hi, I'm a doctor, and I'd like to know how I can volunteer."

Another caller said, "I want to donate money for the team to go."

No sooner would a call end before the phones rang again. "Hi, my name is Rick Stein. I'm an attorney, and I'm willing to come down and empty wastebaskets if it would help."

"Hello! My name is Ed Cameron. I'm a real estate agent. What can I do?"

To our surprise, the phones rang all evening, further prompted by the plea that aired on the eleven o'clock news.

At 1:00 a.m., when the phones finally quieted, Jean and I sat in stunned silence. The response of so many people was staggering. Hundreds had heard the Holy Spirit's call to help the refugees and had been waiting for the opportunity to respond.

For two weeks, the telephones rang day and night. Laypeople and medical professionals volunteered, handling the phones and serving in other ways. Others provided funds. In just two weeks, donations were over $250,000! We were astounded and overjoyed with gratitude, witnessing God's faithfulness to finish what He had begun.

He who began a good work in you will
carry it on to completion.
— Philippians 1:6

It was clear from the outset that the media would play a vital role in the success of the mission. For the first time in recorded history, news media would report live from a refugee camp. Our nation had seen television news coverage of the Vietnam war, but we had not seen close-up images of the mass suffering before.

The media covered it all as we prepared to take our first medical team to Thailand. Television, radio, and newspaper reporters arrived every day at our small borrowed office, asking about our progress and reporting it, keeping the U.S. Northwest informed and engaged.

We felt incredibly blessed to have many wonderful volunteers, including knowledgeable people who helped us make major decisions like selecting medical team members. Many volunteers managed mundane jobs like filing, brewing coffee, answering phones, and taking out the trash. A fantastic aspect of volunteers is the absence of jealousy and jockeying for positions. They're all willing to help wherever needed.

We gained a top-notch medical team of twenty-eight professionals. After the selection process, we had little time to acquire immunizations, passports, and visas, which often took far longer than two weeks. Again, we faced what looked like impossible tasks. Yet this time, I felt there would not be any hindrances to God's divine plan. We had seen His work from the beginning, and I was certain our team would leave for Thailand in two weeks. Any remaining doubts had vanished.

Normal channels would never allow expediting passports and visas. The volunteers got busy with those needs. Ed Cameron drove to Seattle to walk the team's passport applications through the passport agency. Rick Stein jumped on a plane to Los Angeles (on Thanksgiving Day) to walk visa applications through the Thai Embassy. To have every possible moment to get visas approved, he had even camped on the embassy's doorstep the night before. That morning, he informed them he would not leave until they approved the applications. Rick and Ed would also be essential to our future mission projects and serve on our board.

Others volunteered hours to help get that first team into the air to Thailand. I will always be grateful to everyone who responded to God's call. People whose hearts yearned to help the Cambodian refugees had been waiting for someone to say, "Let's do it!" I'll never understand why God chose me to say those words, but had I not responded, He would have chosen someone else. Nothing would stop God's plans, and there were people ready and eager to serve.

I needn't have worried. In God's divine way and time, He answered all my deeply-concerning questions. How would I, a mere business-man, have recruited a team, gathered supplies, raised funds, and found other volunteers—within two weeks? God's plan unfolded because of those who heard and responded to God's voice in them. Until the Thailand mission endeavor, I had not understood the concept, "I can't, but God can."

> I can do everything through Christ,
> who gives me strength.
> — Philippians 4:13 NLT

The key word is *through*. We can do everything *through* Christ. That truth would see me through forty-two years of mission service to those in need.

Watching unbelievable things happen in light of understanding through Christ is amazing. The work is not ours, but Christ's.

CHAPTER THREE

TEAMWORK

God is not unjust; he will not forget your work
and the love you have shown him as you have
helped his people and continue to help them.
—Hebrews 6:10

Teamwork was the backbone of this mission. We bonded
with a single, focused goal: helping people. Every office
volunteer, every person donating funds, and every individual packing for Thailand were equally essential parts of our team.
Like woven strands of rope, people from all backgrounds joined
us to make the grassroots effort successful through Christ. We
wanted everyone in the Northwest to feel they were a part of this
endeavor to save lives.

Like everything else, the name of the Thailand mission naturally
fell into place: Northwest Medical Teams.

We were just days from departure and feeling more confident,
having gained passports, visas, and immunizations. There were no
doubts about arriving in Thailand but questions about what would
happen there. We were pioneers in an unexplored venture.

I had never been to that part of the world and felt increasingly
anxious as the days passed toward departure. Worries were like

mosquitoes hovering and biting me, stealing my peace. *Will the Cambodians welcome us and see us as helpers? Will the team be successful in saving the dying?* Thoughts of seeing blood and the refugees' suffering caused me to feel suddenly nauseated. *Will I be able to stomach what we'll face in the camp?* I was sure that sadness for the refugees would swallow me.

There were many unknowns. *Will there be a place for our team to work and enough work to keep us busy? Will our diverse group of medical, media, and laypeople work harmoniously?*

Our traveling team included a reporter from *The Oregonian* and a reporter and cameraman from both KEZI-TV in Eugene and KATU-TV in Portland. I couldn't help but be concerned about the stories they would report to viewers and readers at home.

The evening before departure, Jean helped me pack. I would discover in Thailand that she'd written little love notes and rolled each into different pairs of underclothes. Her notes blessed me tremendously through the days and nights at the camp. Discovering the first note, I looked forward to another each day, which also kept Jean and me feeling connected.

The night before departure, I struggled to sleep, amazed at how God had moved massive obstacles and led us to the cusp of stepping into the unknown. In the past two weeks, the impossible had become a reality. Yet despite the miracles I'd witnessed firsthand, human nature continued to breed nervousness in me about what we might encounter. Casting all my cares on Him would be an ongoing practice (1 Peter 5:17).

The team and their families gathered at 5:00 a.m. for breakfast at a hotel by the Portland Airport—the first time our entire team met.

Later, when called to board the plane, there were tearful goodbyes with family members. The air was dense with uncertainties, anxieties, and fears. Oregon's governor, Victor Atiyeh, and Washington's governor, Dixie Lee Ray, were also there in support and encouragement.

As I watched each member say goodbye and disappear into the tunnel toward the plane, awe enveloped me. We were about to accomplish the plan God had whispered to me just two weeks before. We had completed the two-week impossibilities through Christ and were stepping into the actuality of God's purpose.

It Makes a Difference to That One

During the flight, medical members wondered aloud what they might find at the camp. "What illnesses will we see?" "How many medicines will be available besides our shipment?" "What diagnostic equipment will the hospital have?" They knew they would treat illnesses and parasites they'd not seen before.

The moment they walked into the camp's hospital, their questions were answered. Like preachers approaching pulpits, each saw where they belonged. Their seamless segue was a joy to watch.

As I observed what was happening, a story I'd heard came to mind. A boy and his family walked along the beach where millions of shelled creatures had washed ashore, displaced and dying. In compassion, the boy kept picking up the shells and throwing them into the water. It wasn't long before his family grew impatient with his senseless effort. "Stop throwing those things. What difference will it make?"

The boy picked up another shell, threw it into the water, and said, "It makes a difference to that one."

Entering the hospital ward, we experienced overwhelming, heart-wrenching moments seeing and hearing the pain around us. Our medical team leader, Dr. Bruce Flaming, gathered his group, and they quickly formulated a plan to care for the entire ward of 125 patients. As the team began working, checking each patient and gathering medical histories, all my questions and concerns disappeared. Though the medical volunteers had never before worked together or treated tropical diseases, they set about their tasks with a vigor that warmed my heart. Their excellent training was apparent. They were in their element and experiencing a heightened purpose to serve.

Patients were extremely sick and in great pain. I thought about how difficult it must be for our volunteers to care for so many hurting people. I assumed the team would become overwhelmed, but I had underestimated them. Treating one refugee at a time, each volunteer made a tremendous difference.

Laughter Is Universal

A cheerful heart is good medicine.
— Proverbs 17:22

One morning, walking into the hospital ward, I heard music and then saw Don Clark, one of our news reporters, playing a guitar for the children. They were laughing and excited amid the misery where happiness and joy had been absent. Their lives had been shattered as they fled their homes in fear to a different country, hoping to find safety.

How can laughter be coming from these little ones?

Seeing how they loved Don's music prompted an idea. A huge pile of wood used for cooking was stacked about twenty feet high. I suggested he climb up and use the stack as a sort of raised stage and sing to all the people. "Your music may brighten their days and, hopefully, bring a smile to their faces." He all but told me I'd have to join him.

To that end, we climbed about ten feet and sang every song we could remember.

At first, a group of curious people stopped to listen, and then the onlookers grew to a gathering of several thousand. When we'd run out of songs and considered what others we could think of, the people stood with somber faces, waiting.

An old song came to my mind, and I asked Don, "Do you remember that old cowboy song, 'The Wayward Wind'?"

"Yes, I do." He strummed a chord.

"You sing, and I'll join you on the chorus."

While he sang, I pretended to ride a horse, bouncing to the tune's rhythm. I was wearing a baseball hat, and when he got to the chorus, I spun the cap backward, made a cross-eyed, contorted face, and blurted as loudly as I could, "BUT—the wayward wind!"

The audience jumped as if hit by an electric jolt! I thought my enthusiasm may have been insensitive until I heard a soft ripple of laughter begin to swell and build. Deep belly laughter suddenly spewed from the refugees like a volcanic release—three years of bottled-up misery finally released. Nothing could have held back the power of their now unchained emotion.

Even though they couldn't understand the English lyrics, they sensed the meaning. After each verse, I'd ride the imaginary horse, singing out through the chorus, which the audience began to anticipate. I didn't disappoint them. I hit the word *but* harder each round. I'll never forget that experience, the joyful release bursting from the mass of disparaging people. As much as they needed food and medicine, they needed laughter to heal their souls.

Later Don said, "Someone caught my attention from the back of the crowd—an old nun in her white habit. Her hands were raised toward heaven, and tears rolled down her cheeks. When we sang 'Kum-Ba-Yah, My Lord' [Come by here, my Lord], I sensed her praying the words for her people, knowing they needed a heavenly touch, one that could only be provided by 'my Lord.'"

New Beginnings

He restores my soul.
— Psalm 23:3 ESV

A young Cambodian girl named Mai arrived in camp, quite ill and near death. She was admitted to our ward, where Dr. Phyllis Cavens cared for her until she recovered. When the time came for Mai to leave, she began to weep and pleaded with Phyllis, "Don't send me back into the camp!"

Phyllis asked why, and Mai told her story. Her parents had owned a successful bookstore in Cambodia when Pol Pot came into power and began to "cleanse" the country by eliminating Western influences. Taking extreme measures, he executed anyone with an education. Teachers, doctors, businesspeople, and other professionals were slain, some for simply wearing eyeglasses.

One day, Mai saw the Khmer Rouge soldiers headed toward her father's bookstore, where her family lived. In horror, she witnessed her parents' execution. She was then dragged from her home by the soldiers and forced to work and serve as a sex slave and travel with the soldiers while surviving on a starvation diet.

When the Vietnamese invaded Cambodia, the soldiers fled through the jungle, dragging her with them for days. At the Thai border, she managed to escape and stumbled into the refugee camp where Phyllis found her, emaciated and terrorized.

She pleaded with Dr. Phyllis, "If you send me back into the camp, those same soldiers will rape me again!"

Dr. Phyllis, horrified, gave her a job in the hospital. When Phyllis was due to rotate back to the U.S., she asked Mai if she wanted to go home with her. Mai wrapped her arms around Phyllis and said, "Thank you. You are my new beginning!"

Listening to Phyllis share the story, I was horrified. But knowing Mai had been rescued (and by one of our team members) filled me with joy and gratitude to God and our team. I was continually astounded by His work through us. We were able to offer new beginnings to hundreds of Cambodians.

Jean and I couldn't have saved the perished teen we had seen on television before the mission, but now God was using us to make a difference. Upon our team's arrival, we learned that thirty to forty refugees were dying daily in the camp. The other side of those grim statistics was that not one patient died during our team's service in the Sa Kao refugee camp. God saved many lives through the team's work, proving that our efforts were His divine plan. Every life was priceless.

CHAPTER FOUR

TROUBLED DAYS AHEAD

"Do not let your hearts be troubled and do not be afraid."
—John 14:27

When I returned home from Thailand, Jean and I continued to be excited that God had used us to help so many refugees. The experience had grown us, and although our lives settled into normalcy, our hearts were changed, and our awe remained.

I returned to business as a successful entrepreneur. Through the years, I wore numerous hats as I started new businesses and bought some that needed help—a catering truck business, a large general engineering company, a radio station, a manufacturing business, various retail stores, restaurants, and others. I loved starting new enterprises. Once a business regained success, I'd sell it and dive into another.

My daily routine followed my father's example: working hard, pursuing excellence, and doing my best. The American dream sat in the palm of my hand. Yet all the while, a battle raged inside me, spurring me to keep my hand open, waiting for something more but never fully satisfied.

Years passed, and my thoughts often wandered back to Thailand and the people we had helped. Etched in my heart were certain scenes I often revisited. I wondered where the Cambodian people's and team members' paths had since led them.

I recalled one of our nurses sitting on a cot, holding a five-year-old boy, Lon, who weighed only twenty pounds. Our team brought him back from starvation and illness. There was such joy in our hearts once we knew he'd survive.

Another memory was of a young father, ill and daily losing ground. Dr. Phyllis and the team were fighting hard to save his life, but their efforts seemed futile. One day I asked Dr. Phyllis, "Will the man live?"

"I can't do anything else for him," she'd said with sad resignation.

I knelt at the man's bedside, placed my hand on his body, and prayed for the Lord to heal him. Dr. Phyllis nodded in agreement. God miraculously healed the dying man! We could scarcely contain our joy.

Sharing such stories with friends, I often heard, "Ron, think about this: What if you had not gotten up from your living room chair that night and moved into action? Would those people be alive today?" Those questions continued to roll around in my mind as the years passed.

After returning from the mission, I tried to keep my mind fully on business but couldn't. The satisfaction I'd had in my life before the mission trip eluded me completely afterward. I couldn't put my finger on the how or why, but the extraordinary experience had changed me. Spending my time making money no longer made much sense to me.

I'd grown up in a family tradition of making money and felt pressure to follow that expectation. Several family members were close to becoming millionaires. I thought, *Maybe after I make mine, I can do more to help others.* I often felt convicted by Scripture that reminded me of God's directive to care for the poor and needy and spend ourselves for their health and hope.

Trying to balance faithfulness to God with a profession that provided for my family was difficult. Little did I know that a major decision ahead would crush my heart.

Who Owns What You Have?

> "No one can serve two masters. Either you will hate the one and love the other, or you will be devoted to the one and despise the other. You cannot serve both God and money."
> — Matthew 6:24

Right after the Cambodian crisis, a friend had approached another friend and me with a plan that could make a lot of money. The U.S. was in a housing boom, and as a subdivider, he was seeing that contractors couldn't build houses fast enough. His idea was to buy 125 acres of land zoned for housing.

We three agreed the plan was a good move. We signed a bank loan document to buy and develop the land at a prime interest rate plus 2 percent.

The day we paved the streets in 1980, the greatest recession since the Great Depression hit the U.S. As hard as we tried, we could not sell a single lot. Everything we'd invested in came to a sudden standstill. I was about to face the greatest crisis of my business life.

Early on, the partner who had approached us with the plan walked away, leaving my friend and me to pay the interest payments. For nearly three years, I had to withdraw money from our family's savings account to make my portion of the payment. The interest rate had shot up to 22.5 percent.

Losing much of our savings hit me so hard that I walked around in a stupor. After three years, we were almost broke. My friend's resources kept us from bankruptcy. He owned a real estate firm and agreed to accept a property I owned and assume the banknote.

When the recession declined and building resumed, I was hard-pressed to make a living to support my family and took a job in sales at a television station. Never before had I felt so alone and miserable. Four years had passed since the Cambodian mission, and I discussed my feelings with God. *I did excellent work in Cambodia, and this is what I get?* My spiritual life was also suffering.

I continued to go to church, mostly out of habit, but God was about to get my attention in another dramatic way.

One Sunday evening in 1983, our pastor, H. B. London, spoke on a topic I'd not heard preached before: "Who owns what you have?"

The message hit me right between the eyes.

As he spoke, I realized I'd only been giving lip service to the notion of ownership, saying, as other Christians had, "Everything I have belongs to God." He had blessed me so much, and I knew I had to attribute those blessings to Him. But I was conflicted. *I earned everything I have, so it's all mine! When the road got tough, I got tougher and held on.*

The truth was that I had not depended on God or partnered with Him but had relied on myself. That revelation stunned me.

I carried my heavy heart to the altar, knelt before God, and asked Him to forgive me for failing to trust Him with everything I had and not putting Him first. I recognized the truth from God's Word in Matthew 6:24 that we cannot serve two masters.

How can God lead and direct my steps if He isn't the top priority in my life? If I truly love the Lord Jesus with all my heart and put Him first in my life, everything else must take second place, including my family and my money.

The beautiful outcome of putting Jesus first was His evident care for my family. He provided for our needs as He'd promised in His Word.

> God never fails. He proves His faithfulness
> when we put Him first in our lives.

Never again would I place Jesus and His power lower than my thoughts, desires, and human abilities. I vowed to God that everything in me would revolve around Jesus and my relationship with Him.

During that time, I learned another lesson: Having money is not wrong—money is neither good nor evil. Money becomes a problem only when we value it more than our relationship with Jesus and relationships with others. People often misunderstand 1 Timothy 6:10 by overlooking an essential phrase: "the *love* of money" is the root of all evil—not money itself (author emphasis).

Money is a *tool* to gain practical needs and, foremost, to accomplish kingdom work by ministering to those in need (nearby and worldwide) and taking responsible care of His church and our families, all of which glorify God.

Many have learned to their dismay that money can quickly disappear, so we dare not trust in it but rather in God—Jehovah Jireh, the Hebrew name for God translated as "Our Provider."

Take this moment to pause and ask yourself these vital questions: Who owns what I have? Can I answer truthfully? Would I still trust God if I lost everything? Is it time for me to bow before the God of heaven and earth and fully give Him all that I have and am, with the understanding that He alone made it possible for us to "live and move and have our being" (Acts 17:28)?

When I answered those questions honestly from a submitted heart, I finally became a willing listener of Christ and His follower wherever He would lead me. I'd had to lose nearly everything to gain everything most important: new freedom of heart and mind, joy, contentment, purpose, and direction that are obtainable nowhere else.

Only months after my come-to-Jesus-moment, powerful feelings welled inside me about the worldwide need for medical teams. I could no longer push aside the conviction that such teams provided the essential permanent solution to ongoing needs wherever they arose.

I could scarcely contain the plan God spoke in me in 1979, which felt as natural as if I'd been entertaining that vision for years. Now the goal would be the same: recruit medical teams and send them wherever needed around the world. Unlike the Cambodia mission, I felt that the timeframe for this global vision would be ongoing. We would travel the world, helping people heal and regain hope!

Such thinking hadn't been on my radar until I surrendered myself, my family, and my belongings to Jesus Christ. Neither was another grand discovery God was about to unfold to me—another beautiful tapestry that would allow our medical teams to work beside some of the most extraordinary people in the world.

God planted the thought in Jean that we ask the busiest people in Salem to meet with us weekly for a simple Bible devotion and prayer. We did, and precious disciples filled our living room every week. As a group, we sought answers regarding God's next steps in the ministry vision of medical teams globally assisting the needy. The weekly meetings developed the group's patience. Seven months passed before God gave us answers.

CHAPTER FIVE

DARKNESS FELL
OVER THE LAND

You, Lord, are my lamp; the Lord
turns my darkness into light.

— 2 Samuel 22:29

O n an evening in October 1984, I was again sitting in my easy chair watching the evening news when God spoke to my heart.

Without preamble, the news reporter announced, "A tragedy of immense proportion has befallen the country of Ethiopia. It is shocking."

The images on the screen leaped out, and I felt as though I were with those dear, suffering people. Emaciated bodies of children and adults staggered before the camera. Long lines of men carried bodies to bury. Thousands of sick and dying people struggled to reach a feeding center but died along the road. Millions of people were starving, and hundreds of thousands were expected to die because of two factors: the civil war to oust the Communist regime compounded by the region's terrible drought.

I recalled images of the Cambodian refugees I'd seen in 1979 when God first pulled me from my easy chair. That massive tragedy was dwarfed compared with the vast number of suffering Ethiopians. My heart broke for them as it had for the Cambodians.

As I wept over the terrible suffering, I realized why our prayer group was still meeting. God had been preparing us for this moment. For seven months, He had been shaping our hearts and building our inner strength to prepare us to minister to the starving and dying Ethiopians.

Our group agreed we should begin recruiting medical teams. Since we had worked previously with World Vision International, I immediately called one of their representatives. I learned they operated seven health and feeding centers in Ethiopia but completely lacked medical care. Once again, World Vision asked if I could provide medical teams for each of their centers, and once again, I said yes to God's call. This time I had the prayers, minds, and compassion of a praying group and the experience of the Thailand mission, so I felt more confident about my answer.

The truth is, I'm an impulsive person. (I can hear friends saying, "You think?") When I see a need, I instantly want to address it. So, waiting for the Lord's answers for seven months had been a challenge. But during that interval, our group had formed a special bond with Christ and one another, and our shared commitment to aid suffering people had deepened. From the outset, we knew that mission field work was our permanent, global endeavor. Now we saw the vision ripening and flourishing. Our meetings helped me stay focused and accountable to accomplish priorities as they came to our attention.

We got to work, recruiting volunteer teams to help the helpless and express the love of Christ in action. Our teams of outgoing volunteers would restore lives and serve the poorest of the poor in Ethiopia as they had the Cambodian refugees.

Several priorities faced the Ethiopia mission endeavor. Rick Stein, an attorney, rushed to the task of securing nonprofit status for our organization, Northwest Medical Teams. Don Wyant provided the solution for needed office space where volunteers could help put outbound teams together. He said, "You know, I might have something that will work for us." He took me to his office building, showed me an expansive room, and asked, "Will this do?"

"Don," I exclaimed, "this must be 1,500 square feet!"

He nodded with a smile. "That's right."

Scarcely containing my excitement, I asked, "How can you afford to donate this much space?" I'll never forget his tearful answer.

"Whatever I have belongs to the Lord. If He needs this space, it's my privilege to give it."

Don also offered us the use of whatever office furniture we needed. He and his wife, Dee, were the first to open their wallets to help finance the mission that would be the grassroots foundation of the nonprofit medical service ministry Northwest Medical Teams, which would later be renamed Medical Teams International. Their financial gifts and other precious donors' contributions made it possible for our group to operate smoothly—organizing, gathering, and sending medical help wherever needed.

While I was writing this book, Don Wyant went home to the Lord. Words cannot describe what this dear man meant to me. For ten years, he served on our board and as my champion. He was always ready to offer his time and resources. Don was the epitome of one sold out to God, always ready to step forward and help. He is missed and will always have a special place in my heart.

Northwest area media outlets again helped inform and recruit people interested in volunteering their time and funds. Every day for weeks, reporters covered our unfolding story on television and radio and in newspapers. Soon medical and office volunteers started calling to help, and our office began bustling with activity. Eager workers participated in myriad ways with a single united focus: sending a medical team to Ethiopia.

At that time of seeking the purpose for my life, I discovered this truth:

> A life without purpose is empty.

I didn't know then that God would fill my life with more riches than all the money in the world—riches from the most unlikely place: amidst immense suffering. Intense hunger, sickness, and pain would become huge parts of my life—and I would come face-to-face with Jesus. He would look at me through the eyes of those He described as "the least of these." (Read Matthew 25.)

CHAPTER SIX

WE ARE THE WORLD

"I was hungry, and you gave me something to
eat, I was thirsty and you gave me something
to drink, . . . I needed clothes and you clothed
me, I was sick and you looked after me."

— Matthew 25:35–36

All the grain around the cattle had withered and rotted in the field. The three-year drought and catastrophic civil war had taken a toll on the land and people. The young owner of the farm and his family were starving, growing weaker by the day.

He awoke one morning to find that his son had died during the night from starvation. The man was frantic with grief and distraught that he and his remaining family could not remain on their land.

He had heard about a place he could get food for his family, but traveling by foot (his only option) would take days. Heartsick, he could not bear the thought of losing another child, so he gathered his family, and they began the long journey.

Within a day, they no longer had the strength to walk, but there was no alternative. They would die along the roadside if they didn't. That knowledge fueled him to keep the family moving forward.

He picked up his two small children, carried them a mile, and set them down to return for his wife. He then carried her the mile. Each mile became harder; his weakened muscles ached as he wondered how he could go on. By sheer determination, he repeated the process for three more days before stumbling into our feeding and health center.

The human will to survive is innate and harnesses a powerful drive to do whatever is needed to live. The determination to save another person is a prime example of committed love.

The young farmer's committed love for his family saved their lives. His story was one of many incredible accounts we would bring home from Ethiopia.

As we prepared for the trip, little did we know that we would encounter many like this farmer, ready to do anything to save their families.

In preparation for the mission trip, we had sought donations from medical suppliers and hospitals. We discovered individuals eager to help, and it wasn't long before we had procured funding promises from all over the country.

Much more difficult was our next challenge. From various U.S. collection locations, tons of supplies needed to be transported to a central hub and shipped to Ethiopia, which meant months before the supplies would arrive at the camp. The cost of airlifting was far beyond our budget, requiring nearly $400,000. Now we needed a miracle to get them to Ethiopia. The answer came from the other side of our country.

My phone rang, and a man said, "My name is Buddy Suggs, and I'm with Eastern Airlines in Miami, Florida. I'm calling to see if we can help you. I heard you're going to send a medical team to Ethiopia. The employees of Eastern Airlines want to do something as a group to help the Ethiopians."

The words of the apostle James came to my mind:

> You do not have because you do not ask God. — James 4:2

I gulped and asked the man, "Can you get an airplane to fly our team and supplies to Ethiopia?"

Buddy paused and said, "Let me see what I can do. I'll call you back."

Lord, is this Your answer? Are you making this possible?

The next day, Buddy called to say he'd met with Eastern's corporate officers. "They agreed to donate the use of an L-1011 [a giant aircraft] if employees can raise the $250,000 for fuel and secure the needed flight crew to donate their time.

I could scarcely contain my excitement. "Wow, Buddy! Do you think that's even possible?"

"It'll be tight," he answered frankly, "but we'll approach everyone here for donations and mount a fundraising effort in the Miami area. Ron, would you be willing to fly here so we can get you on our radio and television stations?"

"I'd be happy to do that." Soon, I was flying to Miami, scheduled to broadcast our needs to that region.

Days later, Buddy told me the employees had raised the fuel money and recruited a crew to fly us there. I was stunned by how quickly God met our needs, and I marveled at His amazing work.

When I told Buddy that our supplies were at various storage locations, he said, "Eastern flies all over the country. We'll pick them up from each location and fly it all to Miami."

I thanked God for the employees and corporate staff of Eastern Airlines. They'd made incredible strides to raise money, the corporate staff added $500,000 more for medical supplies, and there were even enough donations for a second L-1011 and crew to Ethiopia! Their work and giving were beyond expectations!

I thought about the miracle of Jesus feeding five thousand people from two fish and five loaves of bread, the leftovers filling twelve baskets (Matthew 14:20).

I'll never forget the combined efforts of those wonderful, generous, compassionate people. Their heart work brought much-needed relief to the sick and dying people. God bless them.

Eastern Airlines picked up our first team in Seattle and flew us to Miami for our connecting flight to Ethiopia. Due to technical difficulties delaying our flight from Miami, we were there for several days. I anticipated the extra days of sunshine would be a welcome relief from the overcast, rainy Northwest, but the team was anxious to be in Ethiopia, helping with the urgent needs.

The day the massive airliner was loaded brought excitement to the team, though my nerves were on edge with resurfaced questions that had plagued me in 1979's mission to Thailand. *Will the team be able to perform adequately against the significant needs? What will it be like to enter a camp of 150,000 starving, dying people? Can we take care of them all?*

By boarding time, I was amazed to find my weariness and stress had evaporated. I sat in my seat, buckled up, and wept for joy. *Thank you, God.*

Minutes later, the pilot approached me. "Ron, would you like to join me in the cockpit?" Thrilled at the thought, I quickly agreed. Serving in the Air Force (1955–1962), I'd ridden in some big planes but never in the cockpit of such a large aircraft.

Now settled in the cockpit, I felt more excitement brewing. I overheard the pilot say we were within a thousand pounds of the plane's load limit. The weight in hand with Miami's high temperature would affect takeoff. The pilot would need every bit of the runway to get us off the ground. My heart beat faster as he released the brake and revved the engine, and the massive plane rolled forward.

My excitement shifted to anxiety when he said to the plane, "Come on, baby . . . you can do it! Come on, baby . . . let's go . . . I know you can, I know you can."

He was still speaking to the bird when I saw the end of the runway looming before us, and we hadn't yet lifted off. *Lord,* I pleaded, *we need some help here.* I imagined our colossal jet crashing into the approaching fence and bursting it into a ball of fire. That's when I heard the pilot say, "That's it, baby!"

The plane started lifting, and I heaved a long breath of relief, unaware I hadn't been breathing. The plane slowly climbed upward, clearing the fence by just three hundred feet. From my vantage point, the bottom of the aircraft had barely missed skimming the barrier.

During the trip, Eastern's volunteer flight crew attended to our team as though we were royalty, offering extra services for our comfort. But the highlight (after takeoff) was our approach to Addis Ababa Airport.

Seeing the runway stretched out before us, I was thankful we'd made it there safely. A flight crew member began to play the song "We Are the World," recorded by known artists to raise funds for the Ethiopian famine victims. There wasn't a dry eye among us. The lyrics said what we all felt; we were part of humanity and responsible for one another. The song inspired us with fresh determination to do all we could to help.

The atmosphere felt as though the whole world supported us, reconciling human differences to minister in unity to the needy. I was grateful to all who prayed and offered their time, money, and services that made our vision a reality. And I was thankful to God for orchestrating it all.

Give Them Today

> "Do not worry about tomorrow."
> — Matthew 6:34

Once we arrived in Ethiopia, our team was allocated into groups and sent to several intensive care centers around the country.

The first camp I flew into was at an eight-thousand-foot elevation where night temperatures would drop near freezing. The people were ill-prepared for the cold—like the young mother who removed her burlap dress and wrapped up her baby to prevent the child from freezing to death. Each visit to the various clinics unfolded heart-wrenching examples of parents' love that drove them on when all hope seemed lost—like the farmer who carried his family, mile after mile, day after day, to find food.

From the air, I could see the nearly one hundred thousand ghostly figures waiting around the feeding and health center. The starving forms looked like victims of World War II's Nazi concentration camps. Any physical distinction between males and females was often hidden because of their skeletal bodies.

Our medical team quickly adjusted to accommodate the horrid conditions. Within hours on the first day, we realized that nurses would have to serve as doctors. There were not enough physicians to care for the many people who needed intensive care. Nurses quickly became adept at diagnosing ailments.

Two nurses tried to start an IV on a severely dehydrated infant and failed; the child's veins had collapsed. Later, when I asked about the baby's health, Nurse Marie Davis wept and said, "We lost the baby.

It's awful. Every night I return to my tent, get on my knees, and ask God to forgive me for not saving more people." My heart ached for her and the team while beating with pride over their nobility. Our incredibly loving volunteers saw each life as precious, with no regard to race, creed, or color. They saw desperately hungry and ill people and went to every available length to alleviate their suffering.

Eager to comfort Marie, I embraced her and said, "You must not blame yourself. The truth is that God is pleased and grateful for your tender, compassionate heart. He weeps with you."

> When Jesus saw her weeping, and the Jews who had come along with her also weeping, he was deeply moved in spirit and troubled. . . . Jesus wept.
> — John 11:33, 35

Amid overwhelming human tragedy, we embraced the value of humor that helped raise our heavy spirits. As team members rolled out of their sleeping bags each day, they sought lightness in counting their flea bites. Marie laughed as she said, "I counted over 250 bites on my body!" Humor relieved a bit of stress in the increasingly challenging days and the moments of tedium.

During an interview with one of our nurses, the television news reporter asked, "What do you think you can accomplish among all these sick and dying people?"

She thought for a moment and said, "Well, I guess we're giving them *today*. Maybe then they'll have *tomorrow*."

Her words became our team's motto for years to come, printed on our documents and office walls to remind us of our focus: "We give them today so they may have tomorrow."

I was often asked, "Why does the work matter? What can one do among so many? Why work so hard when the people will likely die in the next famine or war?"

In my heart, I could only think we were gifting the ill and starved with a few more days with their loved ones and the wonderful love of God. What more could we ask for in this life?

When I looked into the faces of a young mother and dad who had lost three of their four children, I understood their urgent desire to see their remaining child live and prosper. Dr. Travis Cavens used to say, "I don't save lives; I prolong them!" He was so right.

The needs of others cross all political, ethnic, and cultural boundaries. We must never choose whom we will love or help. God loves us each as though we're the only ones who have ever lived. Our loving God sees people equally and His created colors and other human variances as beautiful.

God created all people in His image (Genesis 1:27). All people came through the only couple God created—Adam and Eve (Acts 17:26).

In a dying African baby in my arms, I saw Jesus. In the face of the grieving Armenian mother who lost her children in an earthquake, I saw Jesus.

> "A new command I give you: Love one another. As I have loved you, so you must love one another."
> — John 13:34

We each will die one day, but between birth and death, we are called and purposed to reach out and help others grasp their destinies—and we will see God in them.

If you want to see others through God's eyes, go out with a mission team. You'll be changed forever after.

King David knew Israel needed to be restored by God. They had failed to live out the truth. David cried out to God:

> Restore us, O God; make your face shine on us, that we may be saved.
> — Psalm 80:3

America has failed God—the One who created our nation as a free people and inspired our founders to proclaim us "one nation under God." We've failed to keep that pledge, but it's not too late for our country's restoration. We must humble ourselves before God and see and treat one another worldwide as one people, one race, each loved equally and compassionately by our Creator.

Without God, a nation will fail. Pray for our country. Change must take place in each individual.

Empty Buckets

> "Freely you have received; freely give."
> — Matthew 10:8

I think again of the young farmer who endured terrible loss and pain and carried his family on foot for days to reach the clinic. I imagine his children are alive today with families of their own. So, when people ask whether our team truly makes a difference, I can honestly say, "God only knows." And I add, "However, seeing the joy on the faces of parents whose children were saved matters deeply to me."

I'm again reminded of the boy who kept throwing shelled creatures back into their life source and saying, "It makes a difference to that one."

There were also life-and-death circumstances in Ethiopia that didn't turn out well. In the camp with over 150,000 hungry people, 1,400 mothers with their starving babies lined up outside the clinic each morning. Each hoped her baby would gain admission into the intensive feeding program. But tragically, lack of space and food allowed treatment for only two hundred of the worst cases each day.

Every morning, our nurses walked the line with heavy hearts, feeling between the babies' fingers to determine the fat content. As heartbreaking as it was, the number of ill people was so enormous that nurses knew some unadmitted babies would die by the next day. The nurses carried the burden of choosing, in essence, who would live and die as parents bore the burden of desperate hope and crushing grief.

Often, I wished I were a medical person so I could better help—but, I admit, not in such tormenting moments. The courageous nurses would complete the selections and then rush to a quiet place where they felt free to sob their terrible heartache. The burdens were overwhelming. The nurses and doctors were there out of compassion and their willingness to make personal sacrifices for the sake of those they could serve.

One morning as I watched the nurses moving down the long line, I spotted two aged women in the distance walking toward me. Each carried a small plastic bucket, hoping to find grain.

They stopped just a couple of feet in front of me, and within seconds, one lady started trembling violently and fell to the ground. Nurses rushed to her aid, but it was too late. She died there, just a few feet from help.

Not long after, a photographer took a picture of her and gave it to me. The woman lay on her side in a heap, an arm outstretched, inches from the other hand lying near the bucket of her hope. All three—body, bucket, and hope—had dropped quickly and empty. I kept the photograph, though her lifeless image was etched permanently in my memory.

> God doesn't waste a single
> moment but uses our experiences
> and remembrances to fuel us to
> help those in need.

The empty bucket is a powerful symbol. There are millions of empty buckets in our world, and Medical Teams International is still working to fill those buckets, emptied by grief, hunger, homelessness, loneliness, sickness, war, and natural disasters.

Today, Medical Teams International serves worldwide, including in the U.S., filling the needy with hope, love, and practical needs. Our volunteers give themselves today so the hopeless may have a tomorrow.

There are now more refugee camps than at any time in history. Medical Teams International is serving in many regions of desperation and death.

Changed

When I returned home from Ethiopia, I woke in the middle of the night in tears, reliving horrendous incidents. I understood what war veterans must feel as they relive their horrifying experiences.

Ethiopia changed my perception of our country's needs. On my return, I found myself more open to the needs of Americans experiencing grief, starvation, homelessness, fear, desperation, poverty, and hopelessness. From my time in Ethiopia, a desolate country of perishing and disparaging people, nothing in me has been the same; everywhere I look, at home and abroad, I see human needs.

As a result, a burning desire rose in me to communicate what I had witnessed, and I became a spokesperson for millions of suffering people globally. Articulating the actuality of desperately needy people to those who had not personally experienced such grave needs and hopelessness was incredibly difficult. Friends encouraged me to speak from my heart the unvarnished truth and believe that God would use my shared experiences for His glory and leave the harvest to Him.

To communicate what was in my heart and the images branded in my mind, I drew a word picture of the lady with the empty bucket. God had preserved the details in my memory, further aided by the photograph, so I would never forget the countless empty buckets throughout our world, the feeling of helplessness, the pain of grief for others, and the miracles birthed from compassionate care by volunteers. We weren't special; we were everyday, ordinary individuals who answered a call to supply practical aid, love, and hope to the hopeless and dying.

We Americans are amazingly blessed. God's abundance over us is not for lining our pockets but for blessing others.

> We are to take from our buckets to help fill someone else's.

Beautiful results blossom when we take steps in compassion, commission, and faith. We find that when we fill the buckets of others, our own is never empty.

> There was food every day . . . . the jar of flour was not used up and the jug of oil did not run dry. — 1 Kings 17:15–16

There had been a time when my bucket was empty. A time when I felt hopeless and believed that nothing could ever fill my void.

CHAPTER SEVEN

A DIFFICULT CHILDHOOD

Fathers, do not embitter your children, or
they will become discouraged.

— Colossians 3:21

As human beings, we have the innate ability to hide pain and scars deep in the recesses of our minds. To look at me and talk with me, you would not know I carried painful inner wounds and scars. I had become proficient at hiding them.

I was born in San Bernardino, California, on August 12, 1938. My wounding began when I was about five years old and continued for years. I have no memories of the assaults from prior years.

My dad met and married my mom in the 1930s, a terrible time in our world's history. Mom had come out of a previous marriage with three children, and our country was entering the Great Depression—the most economically depressed time in U.S. history. Their life was all the harder because they had four sons during the Depression and a fifth during WWII—eight children to care for in a profoundly depressed economy.

My dad worked arduously through the Great Depression with little to show for it and went through a long period of anger. I was too young to understand what spurred his wrath and lashing out against our family. Many years would pass (long after the damage was done) before I'd begin to understand his circumstance and mindset. But his transformation in his later years was a tremendous gift from God.

Dad was a motor grader operator, making about $150 a month, working eight to twelve hours a day. Looking back, I can imagine how the financial stress, the long days, and the responsibility of eight children could have affected him.

I was the next-to-last child. My two brothers, Carl and Wiley, and I received the brunt of Dad's anger and frustration. The physical and emotional punishments he dealt us were beyond normal. Nearly all our family members had to endure his outbursts, which profoundly affected our self-confidence and feelings of self-worth.

> Harsh words that enter a young child's mind never leave. Words and acts of anger permanently injure a child's spirit and destroy confidence, leading to a life of self-destruction.

Wiley took the path of self-destruction. I love and miss him. I knew the demons he fought because they were also mine. Carl became a very successful businessman, but he too fought emotional pain throughout his life. My life was headed in the same destructive direction until a special event changed me later in life.

I grew up hating school, particularly math. My father's discouraging words and physical anger led me to believe I was stupid and wouldn't amount to much. Terror would overtake me when I had to bring report cards home for him to sign. My dislike of school resulted from my fears about Dad's reaction to my grades. My grades suffered from the vicious cycle. I even failed algebra, which bothered me for years until I discovered (at age twenty-three) a night class in algebra and felt compelled to attend. I was as surprised as anyone when I earned an A! Realizing I could succeed in algebra restored some confidence, but deeper recovery and healing would take years.

Mom did her best to defend us from Dad's eruptions. To this day, I bless mothers who stand up to protect their children, though I realize many mothers become debilitated by fear and feel unable to stand up for themselves and their children. *God, help them all; give them the courage to get help and protect themselves and their children.*

Eventually, Mom had enough of Dad's abuse and told him if he didn't change, she would leave him and take their kids. That was a wake-up call for him, and in the end, my parents spent sixty-four years together. Dad had finally made the right choice. I'm thankful to have had a dad who came to care enough to make such enormous changes.

Let me add something important. Until I was older, I didn't know what Mom had said to Dad that caused him to change and stop abusing us, but I'm enormously proud of him for having the strength of character to wake up and change into a loving dad. Many men abuse their families and don't stop, even when they've critically wounded someone. A small percentage do the work to change, but, tragically, divorce often precipitates change.

> To live as a true man is to see your faults and do the inner work to change. Behavioral change takes inner strength, courage, and humility.

I admire fathers like mine who see their faults and change their behaviors.

I'm a faulty human being too, with no way of knowing how hard life was for my dad as he tried to provide for a family of ten during the

Great Depression. I cannot judge him or condone abuse. But I can tell you that my dad became a winner! My youngest brother grew up in happier years under our changed dad, and I'm so thankful.

Who of us can say we're perfect dads? Not me! Only our Heavenly Father is perfect. My goal in sharing about my dad and his change is to ask parents to look at their lives honestly and ask themselves this question: Am I providing a truly positive, safe, secure, encouraging, and loving environment for my spouse and children, or am I igniting fear, bitterness, and discouragement in them?

The Balm of Encouragement

In junior high, I discovered I had a pleasing singing voice. With a newfound sense of worth, I began to sing at school dances and in school plays and choir. The compliments helped build me up. The affirmations meant a lot to me because I wasn't getting encouragement at home from my dad. My mom attended a few of my junior high and high school events, but Dad didn't attend any of my school performances.

> Parents, be there for your children with encouragement, tenderness, and love!

You may think that attending your children's events means little to them, but consider this: Do you remember your parent's level of involvement and emotional support of you? Your children will remember yours, whether they ever mention it or not. We don't forget our upbringings; our minds store our memories, and the darker ones are sharp and painful for a lifetime. Show and tell your children how important they are to you. Both are important, though showing speaks much louder than words. Words without demonstration are empty.

Don't excuse yourself in your mind or to your children with manipulative statements like "I work hard to put food on the table and clothes on your back!" I did not buy such reasoning; neither did you, nor will your children.

The importance of putting food on the table and clothes on your children will never take the place of your eager attention and time, your attendance at their events, and your praise regarding their schoolwork and other efforts.

The following directive applies to everyone—including you as a parent:

> Encourage one another daily, as long as it is called "Today," so that none of you may be hardened by sin's deceitfulness.
> — Hebrews 3:13

Every day encourage your children in every way, and you will see great dividends while they're growing up and when they're grown. What is sown is reaped.

About the time I entered my senior year of high school, my father had an opportunity to become a partner in a grading and paving business in Oxnard, California, about an hour and a half drive from Colton, where I attended high school. I desperately wanted to finish school in Colton, so I asked Dad if I could stay and live with my brother Carl. He'd graduated three years earlier and was working while attending San Bernardino Community College. He lived in a twelve-foot camper parked in a trailer court across the street from Colton High School. The camper had no bathroom or shower, but there was a cooking area, a camp table, and a bed we could share, which was fine since we'd shared a bed until he had moved from home.

Dad granted permission on the condition that I support myself. I agreed and took two jobs. Each morning at 4:30 a.m., I'd go to the bowling alley and clean the facility, which took about two and a half hours. Then I'd go to the trailer court's shower house, take a shower, and head to school. After school each day, I'd work at a meat-packing plant, counting and packaging spoiled hot dogs to be shipped back to the supplier. The job took several hours each afternoon. In case you're wondering, I couldn't eat a hot dog until years later.

After my afternoon job, I'd return to the trailer and help Carl fix dinner. Then I'd study, go to bed, and repeat the same activities the next day. On the weekends, I sometimes visited my grandparents and went to school dances.

Carl was a great brother to me. He had come to my defense during our growing-up years. I cherish the time I had with him. He's passed from this life but not from my memory.

In my junior year, I got the starring role in the school's junior play and loved it. The next year, I was offered the starring role in the senior play, but because of work, I had no time to practice and declined the role. I was very disappointed to miss out on that honor. Consequently, I lost interest in everything. I was so overwhelmed with two jobs and schoolwork, I called my parents and asked to move in with them to finish the school year. Dad agreed, and I moved halfway through my senior year. But because I knew no one at Oxnard High School, I felt out of sync in the new place and fell deeper into hating my life.

Driving to school one morning, feeling down, I did something that changed the course of my life. At first, I merely drove past the Air Force Recruiting sign. But within blocks, the words and implications still held center stage in my thoughts. I turned the car around, drove back, walked into the recruiting office, and asked, "Can I join the Air Force?" I was seventeen and didn't know if the military accepted kids my age. They did and sent me on my way with the paperwork my parents would need to sign for me to enlist.

Arriving home, I saw my mom outside hanging clothes to dry. As I approached, she asked, "Ronnie, what are you doing home?"

"I want to join the Air Force and need my parents' okay."

She looked startled. "You'll have to get Dad to sign, and he might not want to."

As I waited for Dad to get home, my anxiety grew by the minute. Nothing could have prepared me for his reaction.

Mom got to him first and told him I had something to ask him. With trembling hands, I told him what I'd done and that I needed his approval. I was shocked when he just looked at me and said, "Go ahead; it's your life."

More than anything else, I felt greatly relieved that I didn't get a lecture.

He signed the form, and two days later I was on a bus headed for basic training and all the pain that entails. Though the training was no picnic, I felt I was doing something important and finally belonged to something. I also felt a sense of pride in wearing the uniform of the country I loved.

That was the beginning of tremendous life changes that ultimately paved the road to sharing the amazing stories of my journey in this book.

CHAPTER EIGHT

LESSONS LEARNED
FROM THE AIR FORCE

Blessed is the man who finds wisdom, the
man who gains understanding.

— Proverbs 3:13

After basic training, the Air Force sent me to MacDill AFB
in Tampa, Florida. I was assigned an administrative position in Air Operations and loved it. A year later, I was
reassigned to a base outside Munich, Germany. There I worked in
the orderly room—the heart of a squadron—and the office of the
squadron commander and first sergeant.

I'm a visual learner, so I eagerly watched how everything operated.
I managed the squadron's payroll, which gave me close contact
with the pilots and airmen. I wanted to learn everything I could
and even worked after hours helping in another squadron to learn
more. Little did I know that my proactivity would earn me the
Airman of the Quarter title.

I'd been in Munich for a year when the base closed. I was sent to
Wiesbaden, Germany, the headquarters for all U.S. Air Force bases
in Europe, and worked in the Secret Message Center. I learned
so much. Unknown to me then, these experiences and knowledge

would help me later in business and in starting a premier nonprofit organization.

The Air Force was the best decision I made in my young adult years. Learning and practicing discipline and gaining knowledge about organizational principles and functionalities grew my self-confidence from the little seedling in me. Nurturing confidence helped to further my success through the years, but it did nothing to address the pain in my heart.

To parents whose children are not considering college and wondering what alternatives to pursue:

My advice is to encourage your children to consider military service. In addition to learning discipline and gaining job training and experience, young people in military service gain many other fundamental benefits. Very importantly, they will gain confidence as they discover their strengths, weaknesses, talents, and passions that develop a solid foundation for adult success. Military service also promotes appreciation for the country they serve. And, after serving, the government will pay up to 100 percent of tuition for college.

Of course, I say, "Go, Air Force!" To this day, I continue to use the confidence and skills I learned in military service.

Two Big Events

> "What good will it be for someone to gain the whole world, yet forfeit their soul?"
> — Matthew 16:26

Two noteworthy events in my life happened during my time at Wiesbaden Air Base. I worked alongside my buddy Chuck Grider, first at a base in Munich and then in Wiesbaden. Chuck is still my buddy after all these years. We would hang out at the Airman's Club, where weekly shows were staged. Rock and roll was hot in the 1950s. We loved listening to the groups that performed at the club. The lead singer of a favorite group was Gus Backus, who'd sung with a popular doo-wop group stateside, the Del Vikings. The group recorded eight gold records, including the popular song "Come Go with Me."

At that time, all the group members were in the Air Force. Gus, reassigned to Wiesbaden, was a medic and an incredible performer. Not only did he have a great voice, but he also played the piano standing up as Little Richard had. At the Airman's Club, Gus formed a new Del Viking group. They had the distinction of being one of the country's first integrated multiracial singing groups.

I was visiting the barracks next door, wandering down the hallway, when I heard men singing together in beautiful harmony. The door was partly open, and I saw three guys singing. I was in heaven listening to their sound. One of them, Gene Blue, noticed me and invited me in. He even asked me if I would like to sing along. "Yes!" I didn't hesitate.

Another guy told me one of their singers would be rotating home, so they were looking for a replacement. He asked if I'd like to try out—in front of Gus Backus!

Holy cow!

I thought I had indeed died and gone to heaven. As you can well imagine, I said yes.

I was nervous meeting Gus, but I auditioned and got the okay to join the group! I sang baritone and later bass, a fun part to sing back in the 1950s. I got to perform all the Del Vikings songs on stage.

During that time, Chuck and I learned there were cool American chicks who sang in the church choir on base. We thought that gig might be a way to pick up dates. We joined the choir, and I introduced myself to a gorgeous young lady, Jean Compton. Her beautiful eyes and warm smile struck me.

Jean had graduated from Pacific Grove High School in California. We dated twice, and in that two-week time, I asked her to marry me! She said yes, and I felt like the luckiest guy on earth!

Three months later, on August 8, 1959, we married in the base chapel.

We honeymooned in an armed forces hotel on a beautiful lakeshore in the Alps Mountains in Southern Germany. We were in paradise and thought the dollar-per-night charge was a steal. Jean was eighteen, and I turned twenty-one during our honeymoon.

We returned to Wiesbaden and began our life in a tiny two-room apartment on the third floor of a building with no elevator—and life felt great. We slept on a straw-filled mattress and shared the hallway bathroom with other airmen's families. There were no showers, so we had to bathe at her folks' apartment. We didn't care; we were in love.

About that time, Gus's singing group broke off from him and formed a group we called Les Chimes (later changed to La Chords), making me the only non-African American in the group. The other guys, Gene Blue, Bob Brown, and Dan Moss, were great to work with, treating me like a brother. I'm still in contact with them.

A week after we broke from Gus, he called and asked me to drop by his house. "I have an idea," he said, "about translating American rock and roll into German and recording the songs." (More on this story in a later chapter.)

While in Germany, I reenlisted with a two-year contract, thinking the Air Force would be my career. I was rotated to the U.S. and assigned to Luke Air Force Base in Arizona. Poor Jean didn't know what she was getting into when she married me.

We rented a small one-bedroom home in Peoria, Arizona. The rent was very appealing: forty-five dollars a month, including utilities. Unfortunately, the house sat far from town in the middle of a cotton field.

We had one car, and I drove it to the base each day. Jean spent long days alone, crying under the weight of loneliness. Within six months, she was pregnant with our first child. My parents took pity on us and bought us a used thirty-two-foot trailer. And, bless their hearts, they pulled the thing across the 100-degree Mojave Desert, driving a vehicle without air-conditioning.

Dad set up the trailer at a court in Glendale, Arizona, where we found other Air Force families. Life felt much better. Jean became close friends with some of the ladies. I shared the daily drive with some airmen, which gave Jean some days with the car.

We enjoyed time with other military families, like picnics in the park. We all were poor. I made a whopping $250 a month. Our enormous monthly expenditure was treating ourselves to twenty-five-cent hamburgers and a twenty-five-cent movie afterward.

Over the years, those fond memories made me realize that money couldn't buy happiness and that friendships were priceless.

Jean and I still carried the hurts and discouragements of our upbringings. Like me, my precious Jean had a tough childhood. When she and her brother, Jack, were young, their biological father left them and their mom. He was never again in their lives.

Their mom became a barber, earning enough to get by. She had grown up in a church that believed people needed to be re-saved every time they sinned, and she raised Jean and Jack in that denomination. They weren't permitted to go to movies, dances, or even the roller skating rink. Such places were admonished as evil by their church.

Their mom physically and verbally abused them. After she met and married her second husband, the marriage fighting started. Jean was twelve when her stepdad served in the Korean War. His bunker took a direct hit that gravely injured him, and he was one of few survivors. He was flown to Japan for recovery. Jean and Jack's mom bundled them up, and the three boarded a Navy transport ship headed to Japan. Their stepdad survived, and he and their mom adopted a little girl who was half-American and half-Japanese. The three children's lives were quite challenging.

Jean and I believe her stepdad hadn't known how to cope in the aftermath of his service in World War II and Korea. He may have become an alcoholic because of PTSD struggles. Back in his time, the medical community lacked knowledge regarding the extent of war veterans' emotional suffering. Post-traumatic stress disorder (PTSD) wasn't a clinical term introduced until 1980.

Sometime after Jean and I married, her parents divorced. A sad story. Like so many stories we have come to know through our now sixty-three years of marriage, there was a dark time when Jean and I seemed to be in a no-win marriage. We were two wounded souls who'd each brought unresolved issues to our relationship. We were unknowingly rushing head-on toward a wreck.

CHAPTER NINE

A NEW LIFE

Salvation is found in no one else, for there is no other name
under heaven given to mankind by which we must be saved.

— Acts 4:12

Our firstborn, Bill, came into the world the same day
President Kennedy announced the birth of his son, John,
on November 25, 1960. Billy was born in the military
hospital at Luke Air Force Base in Arizona.

Our love for Billy brought Jean and me closer for a time. Bill
would become a fine man, admired and loved by his community
for his service to them while serving in the Oregon House of
Representatives. I can only thank our Lord for that. The anger I'd
harbored since early childhood took years for me to move past and
resulted in some harsh behavior at times toward my son. I've since
asked for his forgiveness and felt his forgiveness. I'm so thankful,
yet guilt sometimes rises in me, and I must remind myself *I'm
forgiven!*

As a husband and dad, I did not make those earlier years in the
Air Force good for my family. I had much more to learn about
marriage and parenting. Later, our two daughters enjoyed a much
better dad because God changed my life.

During our time in Arizona, I met a man who owned a record company. He heard a tape of our singing group, The La Chords, and wanted to record us. The other three group members were still in Germany, so reuniting was an experience that's still hard for me to believe. Dan Moss and Gene Blue were leaving the Air Force, and Bob Brown discovered he could transfer to Luke Air Force Base.

We made our first record, and it hit the top ten on several radio stations. However, we failed to see any royalties and gain traction from our efforts because the studio owner couldn't get the records to the stations' various cities, and eventually I left the group. Later I discovered that RCA Records had wanted to sign us, but our record owner turned them down. Our group hadn't known about RCA's interest. Nonetheless, we recorded several records. Though I thoroughly enjoyed the experience, I had been disappointed and discouraged that my potential music career wasn't taking off.

The remaining guys in our group made more records and pursued other careers. Gene Blue became the CEO of a large nonprofit organization in Phoenix, helping people get off welfare and into the job market. Dan Moss went to work for an airline company. At this point, they have both retired. Bob Brown continued his service in the Air Force and later passed away.

I was discharged from the Air Force in 1962 after six years of service. I feel very proud of that accomplishment. Jean and I decided to move home, where I would work at my family's grading and paving company. We hauled our trailer and family to Oxnard, California. We would face challenging years as our relationship grew distant.

Reflecting on that jagged time, I believe I was going through disillusionment from losing the chance at stardom. Instead of singing, I shoveled dirt, working for my dad and brothers in construction. I was very unhappy. I hadn't yet connected the dots to see that my discontent was related to the emotional issues I still carried from my traumatic childhood. I only knew I felt unhappy—and I blamed everyone else.

Jean also continued to struggle with her past and the pain of her family's broken life.

Our second child, Sheri, was born during that season of our relationship. We brought her home to the first house we purchased in Oxnard. Watching our sweet girl grow up was a very bright light in our lives. She brought us many moments of joy that hovered above the turmoil in our marriage. Storms were brewing.

Jean was in counseling with Dr. Nosworthy from England. He had doctorates in theology and psychology and served as pastor of Oxnard First Baptist Church. Jean tried several times to convince me to see Dr. Nosworthy, but I was opposed, adding to the stress of our relationship. I felt as though we were headed for divorce.

My fear was not unfounded. We separated, and I went to a hotel.

While sitting on the edge of the hotel bed one evening, wondering how our marriage had gone so bad, I became emotional, feeling the separation from my children, whom I loved very much. I thought about Dr. Nosworthy and decided I had nothing to lose; I was losing everyone I loved.

I called him and made an appointment.

After a couple of sessions, he said in his beautiful English accent, "Ron, I would love to have you come to my church." I made up an excuse about accepting his invitation.

As I drove back to the hotel, I wondered what it could hurt to try his church. I called Jean and asked if she would like to go to church with me on Sunday. I'm sure she was surprised, but she agreed to go.

During the church service, I heard things about God that I'd never heard before. Dr. Nosworthy's message explained that God loved us so much that He sent His only Son, Jesus, to die for our sins. He read these scriptures:

> "God so loved the world that he gave his one and only Son, that whosoever believes in him shall not perish but have eternal life."
> — John 3:16

> All have sinned and fall short of the glory of God.
> — Romans 3:23

> The wages of sin is death [separation from God], but the gift of God is eternal life in Christ Jesus our Lord. — Romans 6:23

He spoke about a real hell as the destination for those who choose not to follow Jesus. I had always believed that everyone went to heaven. I'd heard about hell but only as a curse word.

I didn't want to go to the place he described, but I didn't understand what God expected of me until Dr. Nosworthy said, "There's only one way to receive Christ."

He read the discussion between Jesus and Simon Peter that explains who Jesus is and makes clear that we must believe that Jesus is "the Messiah, the Son of the Living God" (Matthew 16:16).

Reading from John 14:6, Jesus refuted the thought that there are many paths to heaven:

> "I am the way and the truth and the life. No one comes to the Father except through me."

That sounded clear to me. *I need Jesus in my life.*

Transformed

On my second visit to the church, a Sunday evening in 1965, I asked Jesus Christ to forgive my sins and come into my life. Suddenly, I felt as though the world lifted from my shoulders, and excitement filled my heart. God forgave me and saved me from eternal separation from Him.

As a result of my decision to accept Jesus into my heart and life as Savior, God restored our marriage. Jean and I grew together as a couple and as believers in Jesus Christ. We both found healing for our wounded hearts, which enabled us to be steadfast through the heartaches of this life.

At last, we shared the greatest common denominator in our marriage: our love for God and our mediator, Jesus.

> There is one God and one mediator between God and mankind, the man Christ Jesus. — 1 Timothy 2:5

Earlier in Jean's life, she had walked away from her relationship with Christ because her church taught that every time someone sins, they need to be re-saved. The teaching caused Jean to believe God was cruel and hateful rather than loving and merciful. She would soon learn that such teaching is not biblical.

Our church welcomed a visiting evangelist for a week of nightly Bible teaching. He taught about God's forgiveness and shared that God forgives and forgets our sins.

Our community was near the ocean, and the evangelist urged attendees, "Take time tomorrow to go to the beach and write all your sins in the sand. Then stand back and watch the tide come in and wash away all the words. That's what God did for us on the cross. He washed away all our sins with the shedding of His blood. He forgave us and forgot our sins as though they never existed."

Jean later shared with me, "I felt as though the evangelist turned on a light in my head; I realized that Jesus deeply loves me."

God had not abandoned Jean; He was her greatest cheerleader. She shared with me over the years that she never again questioned her salvation but grew in her walk with the Lord. She learned from God's

Word that when she'd received Christ as her Savior, God's Holy Spirit had come to live within her to teach and lead her and remind her when she sinned. Living the Christian life is knowing we can ask our heavenly Father to forgive us when we sin.

Jean would never forget this wonderful promise:

> If we confess our sins, he is faithful and just and will forgive us our sins and purify us from all unrighteousness.
> — 1 John 1:9

I began reading my Bible and praying, and I have never stopped loving Jesus! He transformed my heart, mind, and life and is still working to refine me, so I haven't regretted seeking and knowing my Savior and making His love, grace, and salvation known to others. At this writing, my love affair with the Creator of the heavens and earth has been ongoing for fifty-five years!

Over the years, I've often heard people judge Jesus by the mistakes and missteps people make as fallible human beings. Judging the Son of God is the quick path to rejecting Him, your Creator and Savior. I caution you, never judge Christ by the actions of any person, no matter who they are, for everyone is a sinner—that's why we need Jesus as our Savior.

As I grew in my relationship with Christ, I wanted to know Him and everything He wanted me to do. I knew I could learn all about God and His Son, Jesus, by spending time reading and studying the Bible. But I was also enthusiastic about going to church every Sunday because I would gain additional teaching and clarity from those who'd spent years reading and studying the Bible.

I urge you to think of biblical churches as hospitals for sinners. Each time we're in church to absorb God's Word, we grow stronger in Christ spiritually, emotionally, and relationally. Our thought processes change. We grow more caring and loving as we spend time with other believers. And attending church as a family strengthens those relationships and the family foundation. Each time we attend a biblical church, we learn more about God's nature, divinity, love, grace, care, gentleness, faithfulness, promises, and His directives to gain an "abundant life."

> "I have come that they may have life and have it abundantly." — John 10:10 ESV

I urge you and your family to attend church together. When we keep God's Word open in our homes, reading and praying together, our family bond strengthens, is enriched, and becomes more abundant.

A Catholic priest who hosted a TV program in the 1960s ended each show with this: "The family that prays together stays together." I believe that with all my heart.

Each time we read the Bible—no matter where we are—we connect with our living God through His living Word.

> The word of God is alive and active.
> — Hebrews 4:12

Becoming like Christ—inner and outward change—doesn't occur overnight but through a life process of determined will and conscious action in a relationship with Jesus.

Michelangelo's carving of the massive sculpture he named *Pieta*—Mary holding the crucified Christ—took two years. Creating masterpieces takes time.

Our transformations, God's refining work in us, are ongoing as we allow God to chip away at our old selves and reshape us. I'll continue to be God's work in progress because I'm a fallible human. I have times of disappointment in myself. But through my willingness to continue partnering with Christ, He continues to refine me as the person He designed and purposed me to be. God is always refining us for His glory and purposes. The journey with Christ is worth every moment.

My dear friend Reid Saunders has helped thousands worldwide learn how to become free and transformed and have a close relationship with Christ. To learn more, visit his website, reidsaunders.org, or call his mission, Reid Saunders Association, at 503-581-7394.

Looking back on my life, I see the work Christ has done in me. I haven't arrived, nor will I on this earth, but I know my Lord is always with me, always working in me as I turn my broken pieces over to Him.

> Now we see only a reflection as in a mirror; then we shall see face to face. Now I know in part; then I shall know fully, even as I am fully known [by God]. — 1 Corinthians 13:12

Give Christ your willingness and time to reshape you from the inside out. He is the potter, and we are the clay (Isaiah 64:8). His creations are beautiful masterpieces.

New Life

In 1965, I was promoted from shoveling dirt to co-managing my family's construction company. Three years later, a close friend and I started a grading, concrete, and paving company in Oxnard. Around that time, my parents moved to Florence, Oregon, and other family members moved to Salem and Albany, Oregon. When we took trips to visit the folks, we fell in love with Oregon's beauty. Jean and I talked about pulling up stakes and moving there.

In 1969, more new life emerged when God gave us another child. We named her Dawn, for she was a new "dawn" in our life. At this time of writing, God has blessed us with six grandchildren we love very much.

In 1971, I sold my share of the construction business, and our family of five moved to Albany, Oregon. There, another adventure began to unfold. I wanted to serve the Lord through music and started by scheduling concerts. With no outside financial support, I traveled to churches and performed. At each concert, I made available the three albums I'd recorded. I deeply love Christian music because praising and worshiping God in song speaks to my heart

We lived on the money I'd made from selling my share of the construction business, but after a few years, it was time to earn a living again.

In 1974, I bought a radio station in Redmond, Oregon. In 1977, we sold the radio station and moved to Salem, Oregon. Only God knew how that move would drastically alter our lives. In Salem, Medical Teams International would be birthed.

CHAPTER TEN

THE STRUGGLE TO FORGIVE

If you, Lord, kept a record of sins, Lord, who could stand?

— Psalm 130:3

Becoming a Christian, I learned to forgive and love my dad. We enjoyed our time together until he passed.

Still, there remained a huge burden in me (nothing to do with Dad) that I needed to confront to have a heart God would use for His glory. I was holding a horrible secret of seventy-three years.

Jean and I were in our sixtieth year of marriage when I finally revealed to her the most painful part of my life. I felt so ashamed and debilitated at the thought of speaking the secret aloud to anyone. But finally I opened my heart to Jean and laid it all out.

Beginning in my school years, about age eight, I became a quiet child, contrary to how others would describe me in later years and as an adult. A deeply-rooted trauma and fear changed me into that quiet child. In fear and pain, I became reserved, warned that I would be hurt if I told the secret to anyone. I had no reason to doubt it.

Between ages eight and ten, I endured the painful, shame-encased trauma of sexual abuse. I shrank into a dark hiding place within me that outwardly created a subdued little boy. Inwardly, I was suffocating with terror and growing shame, debilitating me from wanting anyone to know what was happening.

> "Stealing a human being's fundamentally intimate core and innocence and injecting fear and shame is to jackhammer whatever foundation of self-worth, security, and love was prior laid."
> — Jen Miller, survivor-turned-thriver and author

Victims of childhood sexual abuse silently and incessantly scream for help—too afraid, ashamed, and buried in pain to utter a sound. Their skeletal spirits—meant to be free and shining with life—naturally seek to be heard and seen by any means.

By the time I was fourteen, a new means of coping emerged in me and spilled out into my world. I morphed from being a quiet boy to the class clown, resembling joy and effectively hiding my secret that there was no joy in me. Deeply wounded, I felt alone and desperately wanted and needed attention. Clowning around brought me attention.

In March 2020, Child USA published "Delayed Disclosure," which included the study results of over one thousand survivors of sexual abuse: "The average age at the time of reporting child sex abuse was about 52 years." [1]

In my case, seventy-three years would pass before I revealed to Jean the terrible truth festering inside me.

Sharing my wounding with Jean enabled her to find her buried voice, and she told me she had been inappropriately touched as a child and felt such shame she couldn't tell anyone.

---

1 "Delayed Disclosure," *Child USA*, March 2020. *CHILDUSA: https://childusa.org/wp-content/uploads/2020/04/Delayed-Disclosure-Factsheet-2020.pdf.*

Parents, family members, friends, teachers, and other leaders: Learn the signs of abuse and be vigilant in looking for those signs! Tell the appropriate person, who will intervene and save the child's spirit and life.

> Sexual abuse changes the victims and often destroys their lives. Be alert to the many signs and tell those who can intervene.

You'll find the signs listed at www.stopitnow.org. The CDC reports, "About 1 in 4 girls and 1 in 13 boys in the United States experience child sexual abuse. Someone known and trusted by the child or child's family members, perpetrates 91% of child sexual abuse." [2]

RAINN (Rape, Abuse & Incest National Network) is the nation's largest anti-sexual-violence organization. They quoted from a 2014 abstract: "One in 9 girls and 1 in 53 boys under the age of 18 experience sexual abuse or assault at the hands of an adult." [3] You can see the accelerated crisis over the past eight years to "1 in 4 girls and 1 in 13 boys." We must stop this massive crisis!

RAINN created and operates the National Sexual Assault Hotline in partnership with over a thousand local sexual assault service providers across the country: 800-656-HOPE and https://hotline.rainn.org.

They also operate the DoD Safe Helpline for the Department of Defense with programs to help survivors, ensure that perpetrators are brought to justice, and prevent sexual violence: https://chat-ohl4. safehelpline.org.

---

2 "Fast Facts: Preventing Child Sexual Abuse." *Centers for Disease Control and Prevention: https://www. cdc.gov/violenceprevention/childsexualabuse/fastfact.html.*
3 "Children and Teens: Statistics." *RAINN: https://www.rainn.org/statistics/children-and-teens#.*

Another credible source of help is the Biblical Counseling Coalition: www.biblicalcounselingcoalition.org/2019/02/15/sexual-abuse-prevention-and-sexual-abuse-healing-and-hope-in-christ/.

Also, you'll find many credible books on abuse recovery at www.christianbook.com/page/personal-growth/recovery/sexual-abuse.

If you know or suspect abuse to a child, teen, or adult, don't stay silent—call appropriate help!

Consider these facts again:

- Perpetrators are often adult or teen family members or family associations, those who spend time within the victim's daily life.

- Perpetrators threaten and frighten their victims into silence. (Perpetrators know the revelation could send them to jail.)

- Regardless of who you are, you are responsible for reporting any sign of abuse so child victims can be rescued, get help, and find healing and freedom of spirit!

If you are a victim of childhood sexual abuse, know that you can recover and live in freedom when you reach out and gain professional help.

I wish I had revealed my secret much earlier. Back then, there were very few options—no broadcasted support for victims and a mindset of not intervening in other people's circumstances, regardless of how sinister.

It would be years before I could believe that forgiving my abusers was possible. But God used a special event to show me how.

CHAPTER ELEVEN

THE TIME TO FORGIVE

Forgive as the Lord forgave you.

— Colossians 3:13

By 1972, I had been a Christian for seven years, growing in my relationship with God. I loved my church, North Albany Community Church. At that time, my pastor, Marvin Jost, was teaching a series on people's hidden, unresolved issues. After finishing the series, he held a special service for those who wanted to deal with their past.

He set a group of chairs in a circle, with one chair placed in the middle, and talked about how vital it was to stop hiding things. "Give every part of yourself to Christ," he encouraged. "Whoever feels led, take a seat in the center chair for the group to gather around you and pray for you."

Sitting on the edge of my seat, everything in me shouted, *Go! Sit in that chair.* It wasn't long before I did. The group prayed I would turn everything in my heart over to Christ so I would be free to live out God's wonderful destiny for me.

After that experience, I was never the same.

Not long after, I got down on my knees and wept, forgiving those who had hurt me in my childhood. When I rose from my knees, I felt like a brand-new creation, with no evidence of the anger and stress I had been carrying all those years.

I know now that had I not forgiven those who hurt me, I would not have God's forgiveness for my sins.

> "If you forgive other people when they sin against you, your heavenly Father will also forgive you. But if you do not forgive others their sins, your Father will not forgive your sins." — Matthew 6:14–15

Had I not forgiven those who'd hurt me, He would not have called me to take the 1979 mission endeavor to the Cambodian refugees in Thailand and all the astounding endeavors that followed and continue to better the lives of millions of people in need. The Lord had patiently waited for me to forgive so He could use me to glorify Him by serving others and sharing my transformation testimony.

Forty-eight years have passed since I forgave others, freeing myself from anger and bitterness. The wonderful freedom and lightness of lifted burdens are difficult to shape into words. I encourage anyone who hasn't gone through this relinquishing process to do so now. Forgiving others by Christ's power in you can restore you from a lifetime of heartache!

To at last live as God purposed for me was a relief that's hard to articulate.

We cannot become the individuals God purposed us to be if we're holding on to anger, hatred, and our wounds, refusing to forgive our abusers and others who have hurt us. Unforgiveness and bitterness are cancers that spread to every part of our being and life and allow our abusers to remain in control of our thoughts and feelings. Why would we give anyone that kind of control and thereby sacrifice abundant life in Christ?

Studies have shown that long-term anger and bitterness can cause heart problems, sleep disorders, depression, high blood pressure, significant illnesses and disease, and other health issues. Anger and bitterness can also cause us to adopt a deep sense of self-pity and build a shell around our hearts. Until you tear down your walls, forgive those who wounded you, and let God heal your heart, you'll not be free to soar and reach your God-given potential—the greatness God has for you!

You may be thinking that choosing to forgive is too simple an answer. Making a determined choice to overcome anything is work, but by believing in Jesus, you have His power to overcome anything! There are many promises of God dedicated to those who overcome. Don't allow your pride or desire to control you and rob you of the unspeakable joy and fullness of God's glory awaiting you right now. Surrender your entire heart and life to Christ and allow Him to transform you from the inside out. You cannot change your past, but you can change your present and future direction.

Perhaps you're going to counseling—great! Keep going. But the bottom line is that only you can choose to change yourself and allow God's work in you. His directive isn't that He will solely change us; His directive is that we change ourselves, which is possible because of Christ and His power within us.

Be transformed by the renewing of your mind.
— Romans 12:2

Regarding my dad, I had an opportunity to work alongside him in construction, and I began to feel a love for him I'd not had before. As I watched him work, I could not help but admire his strength, skills, and work ethic. In time, I came to see him as a hero because he chose to renew his mind and become transformed from a stern and controlling man to a man who deeply loved his family. I can't regain my childhood years, but by Christ's power in me, I became a freed adult to love my dad and learn from him. Over time, seeing my dad enjoy my children was also beautiful.

Years later, I asked my dad if he knew Christ. He said he accepted the Lord when he was age sixteen. I cannot judge whether he had, but he showed a love later in life that indicated he'd accepted Christ.

Just as I would love to go back and change my mistakes, I'm certain my dad wished he could return to my beginning and be the dad he became in my adult years. But the only direction is forward.

A transformation journey can begin in you today—right now—by choosing to invite Jesus into your heart and changing your mindset to become the individual God purposed you to be, a reflection of Jesus Christ, our Savior.

You've likely heard and perhaps said the Lord's prayer: "Our Father in heaven . . ." (see Matthew 6:9–13). Because the prayer is repeated often as an isolated passage, you may not know the two verses that follow:

> "If you forgive others their trespasses, your heavenly Father will also forgive you, but if you do not forgive others their trespasses, neither will your Father forgive your trespasses."
> — Matthew 6:14–15 ESV

The question is, "Can I ask God to forgive me when I don't forgive others?" We must consider Ephesians 4:31–32:

> Get rid of all bitterness, rage, anger, harsh words, and slander, as well as all types of evil behavior. Instead, be kind to each other, tenderhearted, forgiving one another, just as God through Christ has forgiven you (NLT).

An article by Mayo Clinic listed the benefits of forgiveness.

Forgiveness can lead to

- Healthier relationships
- Improved mental health
- Less anxiety, stress and, hostility
- Lower blood pressure
- Fewer symptoms of depression
- A stronger immune system
- Improved heart health
- Improved self-esteem [4]

You may or may not have a friendship or relationship with the person you forgive, but you'll feel the inner freedom of forgiveness.

You may feel there's no way you can forgive your offender, but I assure you that you can because I've experienced "the way and the truth and the life" (John 14:6), Christ Jesus, whose love and power enable us to forgive the worst of worst offenders.

Forgiveness is not only the gateway to your inner freedom but also an invitation for your offender to experience God's love through you and become changed. Forgiveness takes courage. Weigh the benefits.

---

4 "Forgiveness: Letting go of grudges and bitterness," *Healthy Lifestyle: Adult health, November 13, 2020. Mayo Clinic: https://www.mayoclinic.org/healthy-lifestyle/adult-health/in-depth/forgiveness/art-20047692.*

Your present and future lives are worth forgiving others who are no longer a threat to your well-being.

If your abuser has died, I urge you to visit their gravesite and verbally go through the process of forgiving, which will free you from that bondage. Don't allow unforgiveness to linger in you and haunt your life for one more moment because unforgiveness is a prison that holds us captive.

Ask Forgiveness

Perhaps you committed abuse, and the guilt eats at you. You know you were wrong; you've repeatedly wished you could go back and change the past, but you know that's not possible. You can, however, change the direction of your future. Change begins with your relationship with Jesus Christ—the One who forgives all sin and has the power to free you from your past. He's waiting for you to come to Him in humble confession and faith. We aren't guaranteed a tomorrow, which is why the Bible tells us this:

> Now is the time of God's favor,
> now is the day of salvation.
> — 2 Corinthians 6:2

The second important step is to go to the person you abused. Admit your sin in humility (taking responsibility) and ask them to forgive you. There are no excuses you can give when your heart is truly humble. You can't blame your past or any other circumstance.

Don't just ask for forgiveness: "Be transformed by the renewing of your mind" (Romans 12:2) so you can "live a life worthy of the calling you have received" (Ephesians 4:1)—a life demonstrating your changed heart—and you will experience "the peace of God, which transcends all understanding" (Philippians 4:7).

Being forgiven may take time. We can only change ourselves, but seeing *your* changes may lead those you've hurt to forgive you.

Whether or not a person forgives you, know that you have encouraged them to take that step. If they don't forgive, move forward, pray for them, and trust the Lord to complete *your* healing and theirs.

CHAPTER TWELVE

MY LOVE FOR THE PEOPLE OF MEXICO

"Love your neighbor as yourself."
— Matthew 19:19

In September 1985, Mexico City, the world's fourth-largest city, was shattered by a powerful earthquake measuring 8.4 on the Richter scale. Thousands died, and thousands of homes and buildings were destroyed. I'd never seen such destruction before.

Our medical teams responded.

I arrived to assess the need. My Mexican friends drove me around the demolished city, awaking me to the overwhelming poverty. They shared that three-thousand people were migrating *daily* into the city hoping to find work, only to find no jobs. The staggering statistics were six million people unemployed and another six million earning less than a dollar a day.

Squatter communities were rapidly rising on Mexico City's hillsides because many people had nowhere to call home. Families were crafting shelters with cardboard, scrap tin, and whatever plywood they could find.

As a result of the devastation, people were hungry, and many also lacked medical care.

Our medical team arrived and was stunned by the extreme poverty. They got to work, helping those in need. We found that Mexican health workers were also doing a good job caring for earthquake victims, so the medical needs were less than we had anticipated.

I wondered if sending our medical teams had been unnecessary. The answer would come later.

My experiences in Mexico's devastation helped me learn to trust more in God's still, small voice in me. The Holy Spirit speaks to us through our hearts. Hearing God's directives becomes easier when we've submitted our hearts fully to Him and turned our minds inward to hear His voice, and we begin to distinguish between His voice and all the noise in and around us. God showed me that abiding in Him would reveal the course He wanted me to follow at any given time and that His ways always succeed.

> "Apart from me you can do nothing." — John 15:5
> "With God all things are possible." — Matthew 19:26

Successes often come in unexpected ways. I was learning that we're always victorious in whatever we do when we're following Christ. His ways are not our ways. God would eventually answer the "why" questions I still carried.

> When you wish you could help someone but don't, it's
> only wishful thinking. When you dream of doing
> something noble but don't, it's only a noble dream.
> — Unknown

Some causes are so worthy that even our human failures are noble. I believe this perfectly describes Medical Teams International.

Fear of failure can keep us in our easy chairs rather than reaching out to help others. A perfectionist wouldn't be able to feel the success of serving in such devastating circumstances because no mission is accomplished with perfection. But we can give our best and trust God with the rest as we work through His power in us.

> I can do everything through Him
> who gives me strength.
> — Philippians 4:13

What if we had not gone to Mexico? We would not have seen the poverty and needs of our neighbors. We would not have built health clinics or started feeding and training programs for sanitation, water, and agriculture improvement. We would not have helped thousands through our surgical and dental outreach in the years following. The number of lives touched and changed is countless. God inspired, directed, and blessed our humble efforts.

He blessed us in ways we never expected, and we experienced the deep joy that comes only from serving others. We made wonderful friends among the thousands of needy people we helped while sharing Jesus Christ.

I learned that helping begins when one person gets up from their easy chair and motivates others to get up from theirs. We will never really grasp the number of lives Medical Teams International has touched over the years. Yet we do not need to be concerned with numbers or results but with hearing God's Spirit and following His direction.

My calling and yours are the same and simple: take care of the sick, hungry, and hurting, even at significant risk to us.

To laugh is to risk appearing the fool.
To weep is to risk appearing sentimental.
To reach for another is to risk involvement.
To expose your ideas, your dreams,
before a crowd is to risk their loss.
To love is to risk not being loved in return.
To live is to risk dying.
To believe is to risk despair.
To try is to risk failure.
But risks must be taken, because
the greatest hazard in life is to risk nothing.
The people who risk nothing, do nothing,
have nothing, are nothing.
They may avoid suffering and sorrow,
but they cannot learn, feel, change, grow, love, live.
Chained by their attitudes they are slaves;
they have forfeited their freedom.
Only a person who risks is free.
— Unknown

Where Are My People?

> "Speak, Lord, for your servant is listening."
> — 1 Samuel 3:9

On a glorious sunny day, as we stepped out of the van at a dump, a memory from childhood suddenly returned in a flash: I was running barefoot across our family's acreage in California. The wind pushed me from behind, and I felt as if I were running so fast I might take off flying at any moment.

The beautiful memory was interrupted by the dump's children running barefoot around us in the brilliant morning there in Mexico. Not over soft, green meadow but over broken glass, metal, and rotten food. Rather than being touched by a fresh wind, the air was thick with the stench of garbage and human waste, filling our nostrils and sending our stomachs into spasms. When the wind picked up, it whipped gritty dust into my face and eyes.

Although Jean and I were initially in Mexico to assess the earthquake aftermath in response to a call I'd received from the U.S. Embassy, they'd told me more about the devastation and the suspected need for medical attention in Mexico City and asked if we could help. We took a small medical team and set up a clinic. While there, Jean and I visited the dump and were horrified at what we found.

Filthy, tattered clothing hung from the children's small, neglected bodies. Their hair was so matted that it looked as if someone had poured glue over their heads. Layers of grime had discolored their skin. Even non-medical people could detect infection by the mucus leaking from their runny noses.

Rather than on a stunning mountain of foliage and forestry, the people lived in the shadows of towering junk heaps—discarded scraps of all assortments. Like villages nestled into mountain ridges, their collective shacks pressed into the cracks and crevices of garbage mounds. The displaced people had sifted through rubble for cardboard, tarpaper, and anything else they could use to create shelters, as we'd seen in Mexico City. Their floors were dirt spread over the filth.

A pack of mangy, disease-riddled dogs ran by while pigs rooted through the garbage. The squalor was sickening. Open fifty-gallon water barrels lined the front of the shacks, inadvertently serving as float tanks for dead flies. I asked an occupant, "How do you use this water?" The answer was what I feared.

"This is our drinking and cooking water," he explained. "The water is trucked here and pumped into the barrels." Later, I would learn that the barrels had previously contained chemicals, so they now contaminated the water. The people were consuming the water without first boiling it.

I approached a shack, and my Mexican volunteer introduced me to an occupant. The woman was in her forties but looked much older. She'd spent her life working in the dump. She shared, "I'm the third generation of my family to live here. My name is Carmen. I raised my son here, and I'm raising my grandson, Arturo." Carmen ladled some hot, watery beans into a bowl for her son and Arturo. Within seconds, flies floated on the surface. They were everywhere, constantly swarming around our heads and invading food.

As I looked at Arturo, I wondered about his future. *Is this the only life he can have?*

Carmen was one among hundreds of "trash pickers" who lived at the Las Águilas Dump in northern Mexico City. She died a few years after we met, her life shortened by environmental contamination. She had never left the dump.

For decades, day after day, truckloads of refuse had been dumped at the site, and the people picked through the piles, searching for recyclable materials to sell and food to eat. For most, that routine to survive was all they'd ever known. Many of the dump people were so old and debilitated they couldn't walk anymore and hoped a son or daughter would feed them. Life at the dump was a wretched existence for all.

Heartbroken, we returned to our hotel room and wept and prayed. *These are your people, Lord. People You hand-crafted are living in a garbage dump with little food and shelter and no clean water.*

My heart was a mere reflection of God's broken heart. He must have wept as He directed my steps to Mexico City and the dump.

As I prayed, a story came to mind: Amid a tragedy, a man yelled out, "Where is God in all of this?" A voice answered, "Where are my people?"

I imagined God asking me that question. I answered as Samuel had when God had called to him. Samuel replied, "Here I am; you called me?" (1 Samuel 3:5).

In our hotel room, broken in prayer, Jean and I determined to do all we could to help the trash-pickers, knowing the work would be a massive undertaking for our team. Our previous outreaches had been temporary; we'd gone where the needs were most significant, accomplished disaster relief work, and returned home. However, the plight of Mexico City's dump site necessitated a long-term outreach. I wondered if our board would want to make such a commitment.

Once home, Jean and I approached the board. I shared the needs of the Mexican people we'd experienced firsthand. We discussed how this commitment would differ from past outreaches.

Our board has always been made up of compassionate people with a deep love for God and others. By the time I finished sharing, there wasn't a dry eye in the room.

Before we adjourned, the board decided we should do everything possible to improve the lives of the dear, desolate Mexican people. We knew we would need a tremendously increased budget to undertake a long-term program there.

During the expanded mission's inception, I relinquished the notion of ownership and gave to God our board, team, other volunteers, donors, and myself.

As with previous missions, the first goal was to involve as many people as possible, another opportunity for people who wanted to participate in something significantly meaningful. If the mission succeeded, God would deserve all the glory.

I firmly determined we would always pay our debts. As a Christian, if I owed a debt, I needed to pay it in full. How could I be a worthy servant of Christ if I broke my word? Paying our debts was incredibly important—so much so that I vowed I would shut the doors of Medical Teams if there were ever a time we couldn't pay our bills.

After much prayer for God's direction, we planned to take our message directly to people by hosting banquets where potential volunteers and donors could hear firsthand our message of help and hope. My precious Jean spearheaded this effort. Her tireless work involved organizing twenty-one banquets each year. As a result, many people became familiar with Medical Teams, our mission vision, and our heartbreak over the dire needs we'd seen in Mexico. Listeners were heartbroken and eager to help. Their responses were tremendous.

The format of the first banquet was simple: volunteers stood and described their firsthand experiences in the impoverished mission field. I felt extremely nervous about what I would say to the group and how effectively I could enlist their financial help. A friend advised, "Just share what God has placed on your heart." I still follow that wisdom.

In plain language, I asked people to partner with us. The plea was easier than I'd thought because I wasn't asking to benefit me but the wonderful souls we were serving. My confidence grew by candidly expressing my honest emotions, sharing my heart's desires, and asking people to partner with us.

People listened intently and responded generously. Our first banquet was astounding, attended by four hundred people who pledged over $40,000! With that kind of financial support, we felt secure in committing to the Mexico mission endeavor.

Fundraising banquets became a vital tool to enlist support for the work of Medical Teams. At our banquets, we updated donors on the latest work programs and celebrated our volunteers and all the work accomplished because of donors' support.

For years, Jean faithfully spearheaded the tremendous effort of organizing banquets.

Before returning to Mexico, we waited for God to fill another essential and special role—director of the work there. We believed Mexican national leadership was vital to the heart of the mission. We would provide the funding, and American volunteers would help.

We searched for a Mexican director who was proven trustworthy and who would be committed to such an enormous, long-term task. We found that gifted anointed individual—Antonio Vazquez. Jean and I met Antonio in Mexico City and instantly sensed he was someone special. Meeting people of Antonio's caliber is rare. Everything within us said, *This is the person God prepared to lead this work.*

Antonio would become a precious friend and brother. We'd work together for the next thirty years. I cannot adequately express what I feel about this remarkable man. He loves Jesus with all his heart and dearly loves his native people. I'm a better Christian because of the time I spent with Antonio.

This massive mission endeavor launched important work in Mexico City and the state of Oaxaca that would continue for thirty years. God had answered our "why."

Home Improvement

> Suppose a brother or sister is without clothes and daily food. If one of you says to them, "Go in peace; keep warm and well fed," but does nothing about their physical needs, what good is it? — James 2:15–16

Antonio and I had an idea that led us to purchase an old house next to the dump. We called it the community center. Volunteer teams traveled in to add rooms, paint, and make the center otherwise attractive and functional. Showers were one of the first things built. Knowing that children were taking their first showers was amazing, as most had never even taken a bath.

They lined up with excitement, and once inside, their laughter erupted. They were enjoying the experience so much that after a time, our volunteers had to coax them out so others could shower.

I came to realize that cleanliness has a way of boosting morale. In biblical times, a person would get up and wash after fasting and times of deep depression. Washing was a sign that it was time to return to life. In the case of the Mexican children we served, washing was their sign of beginning a new life—a life far more hopeful than they had ever experienced.

We then opened a medical clinic for the dump people and quickly learned that all the children had worms. We immediately addressed the issue with medical care and then started a class to teach mothers how to prevent health problems in their children.

Antonio then started a breakfast feeding program. Prior, the children averaged one meal or less a day and often went days without food. His effort paid off in grand style, improving the children's overall health, concentration, and comprehension.

The improvements were exciting, but the reality was that all efforts required funding.

For the first year and a half, I spent two weeks every month helping Antonio in Mexico and the other two weeks in the U.S., raising funds to continue the work. In Mexico, Antonio and I worked six days a week, averaging fifteen hours daily, to ensure we had excellent programs. The combination of our personality traits made us a phenomenal team, exuding enthusiasm, motivation, and absolute tenacity to accomplish our goals.

The rigorous schedule contributed to the deep bond we shared. I will always cherish our close relationship.

In 1987, one year after beginning the work at the dump, the director of ABC's *Good Morning America* (GMA) offered to tell our story. The opportunity was incredible—a free and extensive platform to shine the national spotlight on our Mexico mission.

The entire GMA crew and a reporter accompanied me to Mexico City's *basurero* (dump). We slogged through the site and stopped to video record a small child with a very dirty face, wearing few clothes and no shoes and standing in a pile of chicken entrails. When the cameraman stopped recording, he wept alongside the producer, their hearts broken. Later the producer said, "We've reported on some very shocking and sad stories, but we've never witnessed such terrible poverty."

The dump's children suffered another humiliation: because they were dirty, foul-smelling, and unable to afford books, uniforms, or transportation, they were refused entrance into the public school system. To address the problem, Antonio started a school at the community center where the children learned to read and write and studied math.

In 1994, something stunning happened. On top of a hill overlooking the dump, a gorgeous school was built, a beacon of hope and guidance, thanks to the gracious gift from Northwest Kiwanis Clubs and Harry Merlo of The Louisiana Pacific Foundation.

Over four hundred children had access to education there. The school was the pride of all who lived in the dump. The beauty and sense of ownership gave the children their first feelings of pride, which helped to build their self-esteem and boosted their hope for the future.

Over time, we worked to bring other innovative ideas to reality. For example, an industrial sewing school. One of the most striking problems among the dump citizens was the lack of support from their men. Because of the miserable living conditions, husbands and fathers were often overwhelmed with despair. Some consequently abandoned their families to look for work outside the area but never returned, leaving their families with no means of support. Other men succumbed to alcoholism. Only a few pushed forward, working to provide basics for their families to survive.

Antonio introduced the idea of an industrial sewing school for women to gain skills for securing jobs in textile factories around Mexico City, thus supporting their families.

Those families' lives forever changed for the better due to Antonio's foresight, our board's support, donors' financial generosity, and the selfless work of our team. Many ladies attended the school, graduated, and further transformed their lives. Graduation ceremonies were touching, not only because of the women's achievements but also because of the encompassing presence of hope in the air where once there was none.

A graduating student spoke to her class about what the school had meant to her. "Here, I learned to walk each day of my life with Jesus Christ. Here, I learned a skill that will benefit my family. And here, I gained self-worth."

After establishing such "home improvements," we searched for additional ways to develop heart improvements. Our Mexican staff asked parents if they would allow their children to attend a children's Bible club. The club was a place for them to play, sing Christian songs, and learn Scripture. Parents allowed their children to attend because of the trust and respect we had worked hard to gain.

The first Bible club began in the Las Águilas Dump with twenty to thirty children. The club soon expanded to other areas, including the state of Oaxaca, Mexico. The number of clubs grew to thirty, with three thousand children attending weekly. A few of the clubs had four hundred children in weekly attendance.

I believe our Bible clubs were successful because of the specific standards we set. Our foremost priority was meeting the people's physical needs. That good work was our initial witness to the love of Christ Jesus that opened ways to feed the people spiritually.

"Let your light shine before others, that they may see your good deeds and glorify your Father in heaven." — Matthew 5:16

Another standard was that our staff never advised the people which church to attend. Our staff attended various Christian denominations. Our purpose was to help the Las Águilas community understand how to walk with Jesus personally as their Savior, not to point them to any particular church.

One of our most important standards was that all our practical and spiritual services were free—not requiring anything in return. From the beginning, no expectations were forced on or asked of the people in exchange for our help. Everything we offered was gifts of love. Jesus never placed conditions on people. Why should we?

In 1995, we came upon Tulti, another dump. The people lived in the same conditions we'd encountered at Las Águilas. To address Tulti's needs, we built a nice community center that produced immense changes for those dear people. We give all glory to God, knowing that hundreds of people would benefit from our programs there, as in Las Águilas.

Twelve years after establishing missions in Mexico, while visiting the Las Águilas Bible Club, I met two sisters who had attended when they were ages five and six. One summarized what the club had meant to them. "The greatest thing that happened to us was attending the Bible club, where we began a close walk with Jesus."

Unlike many children whose fathers abandoned their families, the sisters' dad and grandfather had worked from the dump to care for their family. The sisters exuded gratitude, the first sharing, "Our father and father's father knew only the work in the dump. Had they not involved us in the programs you developed, we would have spent our lives doing the same."

They both smiled, and the other sister added, "We grew up taking showers at the community center! We received breakfast there every morning and took part in education classes. We completed elementary school at the center, and you sponsored us to attend public high school. [A U.S. supporter had paid the yearly costs for books, uniforms, and transportation.] We completed high school, my sister enrolled in nursing school, and I enrolled in the Industrial Sewing School. We escaped the poverty of the dump. We will not grow old as trash pickers."

Eventually, to our great delight, Las Águilas Dump closed. We felt encouraged because we had helped change lives, including bringing hope to the people. Our work there also served as an example for later endeavors that improved the lives of trash pickers in other regions.

The Las Águilas Dump mission was one of the most outstanding programs we were blessed to undertake. Two sisters and hundreds of others were no longer trash pickers and had a more promising future than their parents had. Many are now working in textile factories, and a school continues to educate children who no longer live hungry. Hundreds have placed their faith in Jesus because of the compassion programs we were honored to provide.

The Power of Teamwork

> Make my joy complete by being like-minded, having the same love, being one in spirit and of one mind.
> — Philippians 2:2

The remarkable success in Mexico resulted from ordinary people working together to accomplish the extraordinary. Volunteers did not question God's plans or accuse Him of creating the devastations we encountered. They simply answered God's call in their hearts and took action. *Here I am, Lord; I must do something to help.*

Who were these volunteers? Contributors who believed their financial sacrifices would make a difference . . . caring supporters who prayed at home . . . work teams who devoted their time to building community centers, the sewing school, and the elementary school . . . doctors, dentists, and nurses who used their talents to heal. All were essential in our outreach. All was made possible through the power of teamwork.

The dedication of the American and Mexican staffs was incredible. They went the extra mile (literally) to see Medical Teams' vision become a reality—which became far more extensive than we could have ever imagined. The Mexico mission was then awed and grateful to see previous trash pickers who had benefited from our programs return as volunteers! The expansive power of teamwork.

People from diverse backgrounds, representing various beliefs, had a common denominator: compassion in their souls, proven through their actions. Accountants, insurance agents, truckers, contractors, teachers, plumbers, carpenters, beauticians, pastors, high school and college students, homemakers, and others cared enough to get up from their chairs and use their talents and money to help those in need.

None of those people were ever the same after giving—each gained a more significant sense of purpose and realized who was "the least of these my brothers" (Mathew 25:40): the people they had served. Talking with any giver proved that their efforts kindled a fire in them that could not be quenched.

Evaluating our successes, I treasured and celebrated our victories and teamwork. Such celebrations built our faith and helped us overcome the hardships of later endeavors. As I celebrated, I looked back at the hundreds of volunteers who had cared for others, demonstrating in action the love and goodness of God.

I remembered the volunteer who had cared for a small, dirty child whose eyes were runny with pus. The volunteer's warm hug and softly spoken words of comfort to the child demonstrated his deeply caring heart. Later, as he described what the experience meant to him, his eyes filled with tears.

Until an individual gives to those in desperate need—across the globe or on our U.S. streets and alleys—such genuine sacrifice for Christ is difficult to understand, especially for those of us who live in such a prosperous nation.

Our volunteers understand genuine sacrifice and the rewards of compassion in action.

Standing out in my memory is the return of one of our teams from a mountain village in Mexico. They'd helped the Indians install a clean water system and shared their excitement over helping rid the parasite-infected water and the people's sickness in exchange for clean water and health. Yet the team had endured sacrifice and suffering as givers unaccustomed to sleeping on the hard ground with fleas biting all night, working in the humid heat, or digging ditches down mountainsides peaking at five thousand feet—their hearts pounding and their lungs struggling to breathe.

I reminded a team member that they'd also battled diarrhea. Her response was, "Oh, it was worth it!" Another said, "They helped us far more than we helped them!"

Givers understand the *joy* of sacrifice.

The outpouring of love and sacrifice caused me to look seriously inside myself. In prayer, I again committed my heart, life, and possessions to the Lord Jesus and promised Him I would deny myself and follow Him.

And again, I saw that He answers when I tell Him I'm available. I would realize that none of my experiences from fully giving myself to Christ would have happened—and now been shared with you—without the important initial lessons I learned.

God was about to present us with the biggest undertaking to date.

CHAPTER THIRTEEN

A FORGOTTEN PEOPLE

She opens her arms to the poor and
extends her hands to the needy.

— Proverbs 31:20

"Ron, I've heard such excellent reports about your volunteer teams' work in Mexico City. Would you come to Oaxaca and let me introduce you to the Indians living in the mountains? I'd like to show you their tremendous difficulties." The call was from Duane Marlow, the director of Mission Aviation Fellowship in Oaxaca, Mexico.

His call was in the fall of 1986, and we'd been working in Mexico City for a year.

Through statistics, Duane explained the mountain villages' situation. "Oaxaca is 250 miles south of Mexico City. Overwhelming poverty is a fact for these people. The state of Oaxaca has 38 percent unemployment." Then he added, "I've been flying people and supplies into the mountain villages to help the seriously sick and starving."

The gravity of Duane's voice persuaded me I should go, and soon after, Antonio and I flew to Oaxaca. The following morning, Duane piloted us in a small plane into a mountain village. I'd done my homework reading about Mission Aviation, a group of pilots who fly into the most remote areas of the world on humanitarian missions.

During the flight, Duane explained that the Indians had carved out landing strips in their villages. Some were tiny strips on the side of the mountain, and others jutted out. Flying was the only way to reach the people, except by hiking for several days on a goat trail forged straight up the mountain.

As we approached the village of Las Cuevas, Duane said, "There it is." I took a sharp breath.

"Are we going to land on *that*?" I asked. The airstrip looked the size of a postage stamp—one end embedded in the mountain and the other protruding out over the vast valley below. A massive boulder stood at the embedded end. The landing strip was the shortest I'd ever seen.

About a thousand feet out, Duane declared, "We are now committed!"

Somehow, "committed" didn't hold the typical positive ring. I grabbed the sides of my seat and white-knuckled for dear life. In my view, the plane seemed too high to land. I closed my eyes and prayed, *Lord, into your hands, I commit my soul.*

When the plane met the strip, we could see the enormous rock quickly expanding at the other end. Immediately, Duane hit the brakes. Seconds later, the plane stopped about fifty feet from the boulder.

Thank you, Lord, for landing us safely! One's perception can often play tricks in the mountains.

Behind us, curious villagers were lining the runway edge. Duane shut off the engine, and we got out of the plane, viewing the incoming people from a distance.

As we drew closer, I realized our host hadn't prepared us for a greeting of so many—approximately a hundred men, women, and children. Most were without shoes in the chilly mountain climate. I realized their clothing—torn, tattered, and riddled with holes—was probably the only apparel they owned.

The state of the children was shocking. Their bloated stomachs and reddish hair were instant giveaways of malnutrition or parasites tormenting them, reminding me of the children I'd seen in Ethiopia. However, these children weren't from distant lands; they were our next-door neighbors!

The questions I asked reaped startling answers. The people were growing corn and beans with the same method of faith their ancestors had for hundreds of years, depending on rare rain showers to water their crops. Having no fertilizer and farming the same land for years had depleted the soil. Years had passed with insufficient rain to grow plentiful, healthy crops.

After villagers consumed their sparsely-grown corn and beans, they foraged for food, eating roots and whatever else they could find for the remaining three to five months until the next planting.

These villagers were the starving, neglected Indians of Mexico. Medical resources were unavailable, and no one had come to teach them better farming or how to prevent their health issues. They drank water from contaminated streams and had no latrines. They suffered immensely from malnutrition and waterborne diseases. Their hunger led them to beg us to return with food.

As we prepared to fly out after the visit, I couldn't stop the glaring images of their misery replaying in my mind. But I could pray. *Lord, make our mission effective to save these dear people.*

Duane revved the engine to full throttle and released the brake. The rocky, bumpy runway rattled the plane so badly that I wondered if it would fall apart. Shortly, we approached the other end of the runway, where that mountain's edge severely dropped to the vast valley below.

My stomach was already in knots when Duane pulled the stick straight back. But instead of lifting, the plane dropped off the end of the airstrip and continued falling until the blessed airspeed finally increased enough to lift the aircraft.

Over the coming years of our work in those mountains, several planes would crash, and several Mission Aviation pilots and mountain people would die. We would lose no volunteers.

After we had gained altitude, my mind returned to the needy villagers. I glanced at Antonio and discerned that he, like me, was deeply moved and struggling to hold back tears.

As our flight took us over villages, Duane broke the silence. "Many more mountain villages are in the same condition. Can you help?"

"Yes," I said without hesitation.

Though we didn't have the funds to begin such a massive undertaking, I knew we had to try. Going home and trying to forget the sick and hungry mountain people was unacceptable.

Our board convened to hear my recommendations, and I shared the conditions of the Indians. The compassionate board approved our unanimous desire to help, and we began to seek God's provision for the needed finances.

I sent letters to our donors, explaining the deplorable conditions of the gentle mountain people. The response was overwhelming enthusiasm. Calling Antonio, I joyfully announced, "We can get to work on this endeavor!"

The Indians' most pressing need was food. Duane agreed to fly sacks of corn, beans, and rice to the villages. The flights continued for about six months, when new crops were mature enough to harvest. With each delivery, the villagers voiced their sincere thanks to Duane.

We then flew medical volunteer teams into the mountains, and they backpacked from village to village, treating the people for parasites and respiratory ailments. The volunteers reported that dental problems were rampant. The Indians suffered from abscesses and various infections.

In response, we sent volunteer dental teams. The plan they devised to attend to the needs more efficiently was rather comical. They gathered the villagers into large circles and moved from one to the next, anesthetizing gums and pulling rotten teeth. The people, having never had dental work, were confused but incredibly amazed and grateful when their pain suddenly ended.

Once home, Dr. Richard Imholte, a volunteer dentist, shared a story with the audience at one of our fundraising banquets illustrating the generosity of impoverished people. "At the first village, when we completed our mission, we were amazed that the villagers gathered to say goodbye with gifts, like eggs or a chicken."

He paused a moment. "Our team had arrived in the mountains well supplied—we didn't need food, especially from starving people. The situation was awkward and touching. Their food offerings and deeply heartfelt gratitude were all they had.

"It wasn't long before we realized that refusing their gifts would be insulting, so we quickly devised a strategy. We'd accept the food and carry it to the next village, where we'd identify the poorest families and give them the food." He smiled and added, "The plan worked well until we arrived at the last village. We had given away most of the food from the previous village when we noticed a widow with several children. She lived in a typical hut of mud walls, a thatched roof, and dirt floors. There was nothing on her shelves except two eggs.

"We gave her our little remaining food—a half loaf of bread, a half box of pancake flour, and a can of hot peppers—scraps to us but a feast to her. We left feeling blessed and pleased to have gifted all we had. We then walked toward the landing strip to travel home. We'd walked only about fifty feet when we heard the widow's voice and turned. She stood with her hand outstretched, extending the two eggs." Silence pervaded the banquet room.

"We didn't know how to respond to her. She desperately needed the eggs, and we were headed home to plenty of eggs. We looked at each other with tears in our eyes."

The dentist stopped there and returned to his seat. Amid the silence was a whispered question from the team. "What would you have done?"

I've often thought of that story and wondered what I would have done. I admired the widow and knew that Jesus would one day commend her as He'd commended the widow in Luke 21:1–4.

Jesus saw the rich putting their gifts into the temple treasury. He also saw a poor widow put in two tiny copper coins. "I tell you the truth," he said, "this poor widow has put in more than all the others. All these people gave their gifts out of their worth; but she out of her poverty put in all she had to live on."

Following the dental outreach, we chose people from each village to board at our training center so we could teach them how to grow vegetables year-round for a more balanced diet.

We also taught them basic medical care and preventative health care. They would return to their villages and teach their people what they'd learned. The training program reduced malnutrition and improved the health of the mountain Indians.

We sent teams to the villages to work alongside the people to install clean water systems. As a result, 80 percent of their illnesses disappeared.

Other teams built latrines and made additional simple but dramatic improvements.

When we said yes to God's plans, He allowed us to participate in the *joy* of giving. We had helped not only the village Antonio and I had first visited but also hundreds of communities in the mountains of Oaxaca. When God oversees the plans, they cannot fail.

CHAPTER FOURTEEN

THE OUTCASTS

Hope deferred makes the heart sick, but
a longing fulfilled is a tree of life.

— Proverbs 13:12

In 1987, Antonio and I met with a Mexican plastic surgeon who described another rampant condition in Oaxaca.
"Approximately five thousand children suffer from cleft lips
and palates, and there are not enough doctors to perform the corrective surgery." He added, "My brother and I are the only plastic
surgeons in the state. We don't charge for some surgeries but can't
handle all the needs."

"Why are there so many?" I asked.

"Because the people live in small villages where intermarriage is
common, producing genetic abnormalities," he explained. "I often
see two or three people in the same family with cleft palates. Some
children die young because a hole in the palate prevents them from
sucking their mother's milk."

The suffering saddened me—all the more as I thought about how
easily such surgery is performed in the U.S. during a child's infancy
and the cost covered by insurance or government funds allocated
for that purpose.

The surgeon continued, "Oaxaca children with this problem are usually hidden in their huts and treated as outcasts. Some villagers are superstitious, believing the disfigurement is a punishment from God. The children may not play with other children or go to school, and many don't consider marriage. They struggle with all these issues into old age because they have no other options." He asked, "Can you send teams of plastic surgeons to help? It would dramatically change the lives of many people."

Without considering the practicalities, I said yes, believing God would want us to do all we could for the debilitated outcast children.

You may question the wisdom of my quick responses and may be thinking, *Wait a minute, Ron. You go around the world, saying yes before even raising a dime to make it happen? What's with that?*

I can sum it up in one word: *faith.*

I believe the Bible's vast number of verses about faith. For example, God's definition of faith:

> Faith is being sure of what we hope for. It is being sure of what we do not see. — Hebrews 11:1 NIRV

I have faith that Jesus Christ is the Savior of the world.

Because of my faith and growth in Christ, I no longer questioned my calling. I had faith that Jesus would be there and provide the wisdom and resources whenever someone answered His call to serve.

We never started a single program with funds on hand to accomplish it. Yet time after time, God produced the funding required. God is good! He never fails to provide for His servants, and He always smooths the bumps for us to complete His purposes.

We Can Do It!

> Be on your guard; stand firm in the faith; be
> courageous; be strong. Do everything in love.
> — 1 Corinthians 16:13–14

We faced a big hurdle: Where would the surgeries be performed? The Mexican hospitals had limited space and equipment. And, of course, I had no idea what we would need. But I knew we had enthusiastic people at home who would help me find answers.

I called Dr. Jerry Becker and Jim Bowlin, medical volunteers who had helped after the El Salvador earthquake. I shared the villagers' needs, and they came up with a great idea: a customized van converted into a mobile operating room.

Jim said he and Jerry owned a fifth-wheel trailer that could store our medical supplies and be converted into a surgery room. Amazing!

We soon found a truck, and though it was old, it was in excellent condition and had a new engine.

By then, I was weary from traveling to Mexico and back every two weeks and spending the alternate two weeks raising funds. Whenever I faced the idea of completing this project, I felt shaky inside, as if burnout were right around the corner. I took my weariness to God in prayer, and it wasn't long before I met Doug Rawlins.

Doug entered my office and asked how his church could be of service to Medical Teams. As we talked, he shared that he and his wife, Pam, had been part of the Peace Corps team working in Guatemala, and Pam spoke fluent Spanish. Even before he left my office, I asked him to consider coming on staff to lead this new mission in Mexico.

He went home and consulted with Pam, who said, "Doug, if you don't take that job, I will!" Not long afterward, Doug called and agreed. He was God's clear answer to prayer, a productive and diligent fellow laborer who became a beloved friend.

Doug's first priority was transforming the truck and van into a mobile operating room. He enlisted the help of local volunteers, who did the carpentry and installed the medical equipment. When it was completed, volunteers drove the mobile unit the three thousand miles to Oaxaca.

We took advantage of the trailer Dr. Becker and Jim Bowlin donated by turning it into our medical storage in Oaxaca.

One day, Doug received a call from Dr. Bob Demuth, the director of plastic surgery for Oregon Health Science University in Portland. Dr. Demuth said, "I've heard about Mexico's need for plastic surgeons. Can I help?"

Our God is faithful.

Like an angel of the Lord, Dr. Demuth arrived with a detailed plan to put all the pieces together. Once he and Doug had decided on the procedure and collected the needed tools and surgical team, they recruited medical professionals for the work. Dr. Demuth volunteered to lead the team to Mexico. He even occasionally traveled alone to perform surgeries in Mexico and other countries.

For three years, hundreds of corrective surgeries were performed by compassionate doctors in the mobile surgery unit, transforming children's facial disfigurements and their lives. We often marveled at the dramatic change after a ninety-minute operation!

A young couple arrived with their two-month-old son, who had a cleft lip and palate. Their fear was apparent when they asked if we could help "so he could be like other children." Ninety minutes later, their eyes shone with grateful tears, reflecting their joy and new hope for their beloved son's future.

A year later, the couple had another child born with the same defect, and we addressed his needs. I was there both times and had the pleasure of meeting the parents again. They eagerly shared that their children could now attend school and participate in activities with other children. They expressed their gratitude for our help in changing their children's destinies.

A dad brought his fourteen-year-old daughter to the surgical van. She had a bilateral cleft lip, which meant she had no upper lip except for a small section below her nose. The dad confessed how ashamed he felt. "I believe I must have offended God and should have behaved differently," confirming the long-held superstition of many villagers. Our staff assured the father that God did not do this to his child, but He had sent people to help her.

The team performed the surgery, and it was a tremendous success. A year and a half later, I saw the girl walking with her dad. She'd blossomed into a beautiful young lady. Though she was still shy, we could see how pleased she was with her appearance. Her dad was also immensely proud. Wearing a wide smile, he said, "She's in eighth grade and doing well. She can marry and have a happy life!"

Our team also performed surgeries on older people. One man was in his sixties when he approached the van. When his surgery was over, a nurse gave him a mirror. He looked at himself, and his eyes widened. He exclaimed, "Oh, now I can take a wife!"

We wept as we smiled, grateful for the chance to change another life but saddened because the surgery opportunity hadn't been available earlier in his life. I couldn't help thinking, *If only* . . . But I quickly remembered there is no "if only" with God, and I changed my thoughts to align with His.

We must refuse to be paralyzed by what we see, refuse regret of prolonged timing, and be excited and grateful to be part of changing lives.

The Blind Shall See

"One thing I do know. I was blind but now I see!"
— John 9:25

Years after we started the cleft palate surgeries, we learned of a tragedy affecting the elderly. Thousands were blind and many others were going blind from cataracts. With no help available, the people had resigned themselves to living in darkness. The villagers had no retirement funds or other support like Social Security and Medicare. They felt unworthy and ashamed to be a burden to their families.

Antonio, Doug, and I discussed the problem and agreed that the surgery truck, already in Oaxaca, could also be used for cataract surgeries.

Doug recruited Dr. Roger David and Dr. Bill Pendergast of Oregon City, Oregon, who advised him on the best procedure to remove cataracts. The doctors helped Doug develop a plan and gather the necessary supplies. Then the two eye surgeons led the first team for eye surgeries from the mobile clinic, blazing a trail that other teams would follow.

The sacrifices of our surgery teams kept the cost down to $137 per person. Teamwork and donations were the keys. Team members donated their professional time and paid for their own travel, lodging, and meals.

Working together, a group can accomplish far more than anyone working alone. Hundreds of eyes could finally see again because of volunteers' teamwork, time, skills, and donations to help restore the sight of the Indians.

Being present for the removal of an eye patch was incredibly exciting. We couldn't help but weep with joy when the formerly blind person opened their eyes and saw loved ones for the first time in years. Though I'd been present for many marvelous reveals, the experience never grew old.

There are many stories. Fredrico had been blind for twenty years when his son led him into our mobile clinic for surgery.

When the bandage was removed, the doctor asked him, "Can you see?"

Fredrico paused, blinking, and exclaimed, "Yes! I see people in front of me!"

His son stepped into view, and the doctor asked Fredrico, "Do you know this man?"

Fredrico stared at the man and replied no. His son had been age fourteen when Fredrico went blind. He had not seen his son in twenty years! His son spoke, and Fredrico cried, "It's my son!" We all laughed and cried.

While writing this book, a missionary couple we support contacted me. Martha and Brent Trent have worked in Oaxaca, Mexico, for many years. Martha sent me a story she heard that had taken place twenty-five years earlier:

> A mother told me her family had heard about the medical team doing cleft lip and palate surgeries in Oaxaca. Their five-year-old son had a severe cleft lip and palate. They walked hours to the closest town to catch a bus and traveled another nine hours to the surgery center.
>
> The volunteer medical team operated on young Eliseo Lopez Dolores. Now he has a family and plays the trumpet, which would have been impossible without the surgery!
>
> His mother told me that their whole family accepted Christ and are very involved in serving their church.

We don't always hear updates years after our work, so to hear about Eliseo's thriving life was such a blessing!

What you do today in reaching out to help someone can create long-lasting blessings for the person. You may not see the results, but our heavenly Father does. Serving those in need, you're building up heavenly treasure—the only treasure we'll have from this world.

God's Hands

> "I tell you the truth, anyone who believes in me will do the same works I have done, and even greater works, because I am going to be with the Father. You can ask for anything in my name, and I will do it!" — John 14:12–13

I admit I had been confused in the past by the above Scripture passage. I wondered how we could do greater deeds than Jesus had. He'd fed over five thousand people with only five loaves of bread and a couple of fish. He'd healed the sick, given sight to the blind, healed the lame to walk, and even raised the dead!

After experiencing many miracles of Christ in the lives of the Indians through human hands, I understood John 14:12–13. The Holy Spirit of God worked through our volunteer medical teams to bring sight and other restorations to thousands of individuals.

As believers in Jesus Christ, we should focus on these phrases: "anyone who believes in me" and "ask . . . in my name." God's plan all along was to do great things through His people.

I've since had a thirty-year love affair with the people of Mexico. Medical Teams partnered with our wonderful brothers and sisters there for many years. I appreciate how our Mexican staff loved and treated their people through our programs. The humble people of the small mountain villages of Oaxaca have continued to be part of my heart. I love them very much.

God had again touched countless people's hearts, who responded by providing funds, time, skills, and effort. Each is among those Jesus described as anyone who has faith. God's intentions prevailed: through our combined efforts, He did more miracles in Mexico than Christ performed on earth, and His words and purpose for humankind continue to ring true today.

A statue of Jesus stood in front of a church in San Diego, California. One morning, people discovered vandals had broken off the statue's hands. Shaking their heads, the residents made plans to repair the damage. However, the next morning, they found a sign propped up against the statue that read, "I have no hands but your hands." Truer words were never written. Jesus said this:

> I tell you, whatever you did for one of the least of these brothers and sisters of mine, you did for me. . . . For I was hungry and you gave me nothing to eat, I was thirsty and you gave me nothing to drink, I was a stranger and you did not invite me in, I needed clothes and you did not clothe me, I was sick and in prison and you did not look after me.

— Matthew 25:40–43

We are truly Jesus's hands! As such, we should use them as He would, reaching out to the poor and suffering with help, healing, and love with no biases or conditions. The Lord loves every individual and grieves when they hurt. He was the first and best example of what it means to care for others.

Thousands have caught the vision to be Jesus's hands to those in need. When vision-seers reach out, there are fewer hungry and sick people in our world. God made a promise to those who act on their compassion for others:

> Whoever is kind to the poor lends to the Lord, and he will reward them for what they have done. — Proverbs 19:17

For You, Lord

As I stood in the wings of that New Orleans stage in 1994 to receive the Kiwanis World Service Medal in New Orleans, I felt overwhelmed and humbled, realizing I would be the only person in the entire world that year to receive the honor.

The medal was first awarded in 1985, purposed to recognize individuals whose dedication to altruistic services inspired others. Among notable recipients were Nancy Reagan and Audrey Hepburn.

I was in disbelief and awe to join the group as the tenth recipient. Even today, I find myself asking God, "Why me?" And He reminds me that successes are because of His might, not mine or others. I like it that way.

> "As the heavens are higher than the earth, so are my ways higher than your ways and my thoughts than your thoughts." — Isaiah 55:9

> "I know the plans I have for you," declares the Lord, "plans to prosper you and not to harm you, plans to give you hope and a future." — Jeremiah 29:11

The award carried a $10,000 grant, which I signed over to the mission toward God's ongoing plans to give hope and a future to thousands of people in need. He gave me a wonderful opportunity through the award to represent all who had given themselves to help others through Medical Teams International. They are the heroes, and I haven't taken the honor lightly. I also felt blessed by the honor because Kiwanis International represents civic clubs that minister worldwide to those in need. Teamwork.

Jean and I attended the award event together. Beforehand, we spent time in prayer, simply asking that Jesus would receive the glory.

Nearly thirteen thousand people representing over one hundred countries were seated in the enormous auditorium. I was frightened that I would soon walk from the shadows to speak to so many people. At first sight of the immense crowd, I had said urgently to Jean, "Honey, let's go back to our room!"

In her inimitable way, she said, "You'll be fine." Then she reminded me, "Just give God the glory."

I waited anxiously as the president of Kiwanis International shared a short message and then showed a video about the work of Medical Teams International. My heart beat faster when he said, "Please welcome the 1994 Kiwanis World Service Medal recipient, Dr. Ronald Post."

As I walked to the front, the sea of people stood applauding. The president shook my sweaty hand and stepped aside for me to take the podium. Facing the generous crowd, I smiled and said nervously, "Wow! Your response is humbling, and this check is wonderful."

After a pause, I continued from my heart. "Putting first things first, I offer this award to the Lord Jesus Christ as a gift of praise. Second, I wish to acknowledge this medal and most generous check on behalf of the thousands of medical and lay volunteers who have given their time and resources to serve the poorest of the poor. I must thank our wonderful staff, our volunteers, and our board of directors. Their combined skills made us what we are today."

The audience rose in a second ovation, and I pointed to heaven and offered the award to Jesus.

Feeling God's presence beside me in the reverberation of applause, I tried to fight my tears. With overflowing joy and wonder, I lifted my head toward heaven, acknowledging my heavenly Father, who makes all things possible. "This is for you, Lord!" I raised the award to Him.

Medical Teams had always belonged to God and been operated by ordinary, wonderful people who had answered His call to serve "the least of these"—the poor and needy.

Every individual who had worked so hard with Medical Teams to make a difference in our world shared the award. All praise belongs to God. He devised each mission, called each volunteer, and blessed the work of our hands.

I was not at the end of my journey. God had many more plans ahead for Medical Teams.

CHAPTER FIFTEEN

SEARCHING FOR LAND

I have come down ... to bring them ... into a good and spacious land, a land flowing with milk and honey.

— Exodus 3:8

O ur outreach in Mexico had settled into a comfortable routine. We named the mission Manos de Ayuda, meaning Helping Hands, and Antonio Vasquez was named president. Medical Teams continued to meet needs in various locations. Surgeries were still done from our mobile unit and medical care from our clinic about three miles from Oaxaca. A Mexican doctor we'd hired directed the clinic, caring for the poor of St. Augustine. The clinic also continued to serve as our training center, where mountain villagers learned about health issues, health care, and basic agriculture.

The mission's success produced two challenges: the number of students had outgrown the building, and the surgical van could no longer accommodate the increasing number of patient needs. We needed a larger facility.

If we bought three acres of land, we could build a surgery center and a school for health and agriculture students and have land to grow demonstration gardens for students to see effective mini-gardening methods.

Not surprisingly, we didn't have the funds to launch such a vision, though the need was unmistakable.

I asked Antonio to search for undeveloped land in the city based on my estimation that $6,000 would purchase three acres.

I had grossly underestimated the cost.

Antonio's homework revealed that Americans retiring to the area had increased city property value to a whopping $30,000 an acre! There was no way we could afford three acres.

I asked Antonio to look for one-acre plots, which would work but be a tight fit for our vision. He called with several properties to show me. I invited Doug Rawlins and a staff member, and we flew to Mexico.

Antonio drove us to various one-acre sites, but none felt suitable for our needs. A property near the airport seemed like a perfect place to build, but that site also felt wrong. We wondered if we should trust our feelings and dismiss the properties. We felt disconcerted, having run out of options.

Then Antonio had an afterthought. "There's one more property we could consider, but it's twenty miles outside the city."

Twenty miles is much too far, I thought. *Why would we want a place that far from the city?* However, I agreed to check it out. *It can't hurt to look.*

Driving the twenty miles, we seemed to be in the middle of nowhere. The landscape looked like a high desert.

Eventually, we turned off the main road onto a dirt road and traveled about half a mile to the location. Antonio walked the property line, giving us perspective, and I was stunned at the massive size. "Antonio, this must be twenty acres!"

"No, Señor, it's thirty acres."

What? We can't even afford three acres. I wondered what we were doing there. *How can we even think about buying thirty?*

"There's a well," Antonio interrupted my thoughts. "Would you like to see it?"

"Sure," I answered, wanting to honor his search efforts.

We drove to the well, located in the middle of the acreage. The water was just eighteen feet below ground—amazing since the area was like a desert. But my mind could not see beyond the looming price of thirty acres. *How could we ever afford such a place?* Earlier, when we'd turned off the main road, Antonio had pointed out a two-acre parcel priced at $40,000, and I'd felt my anxiety rising.

Holy Ground

> "Take off your sandals, for the place where you are standing is holy ground." — Exodus 3:5

On the drive to the well, I'd seen holes dug in the ground. Being a former construction contractor, I was curious about their purpose. While the other men went to further examine the well, I asked Antonio to pick me up on their way out. I wanted to walk a distance to check out the ground holes.

Arriving at the other side of the property, I realized the holes were to pull up the thorny tree-like plants. I was on one knee looking into a hole when I noticed a twig about nine inches long, covered with long thorns. The stem of thorns reminded me of the cruel crown of thorns the Roman soldiers had pressed into Jesus's head at His crucifixion. I couldn't imagine the excruciating pain He'd suffered on my behalf. How little those Roman soldiers had known about the One they crowned with thorns. They had attempted to humiliate the very Son of God in the flesh.

Christ could have easily called ten thousand angels to rescue Him, yet He endured the pain to offer all of humanity eternal salvation. *He'd suffered excruciating pain and death for me!*

I felt overcome, unworthy of His great sacrifice. Despite my sin and flaws, Jesus gave His life for me. *The Maker of heaven and earth loves me that much!*

At that moment, as tears ran down my face, the field became a sanctuary, and I felt God's presence as never before. I wanted to wrap my arms around Jesus and tell Him how much I loved Him for what He'd suffered and sacrificed to save me. Joy filled my heart, and I wanted to shout it to the world.

My companions arrived, and I told them about the thorns and my encounter. "I don't know why we came to this property, nor what the Lord's plans are, but I feel we should praise Him." We joined hands and wept as we praised the Lord together. Time seemed to stand still as we lifted our voices in gratitude to God. I had never before felt as I did in those moments.

Beyond any doubt, we were standing on holy ground.

God's Response

> I will extol the Lord at all times; his praise will always be on my lips. — Psalm 34:1

As we drove away, Antonio asked, "Do you want to speak to the property owner?" Something inside me said yes.

We arrived in the city and visited the owner, a Mexican doctor, who shared that his wife was from Spain and had become homesick. She had returned to Spain, and he was clearing up his affairs to join her there.

Antonio asked him how much he needed for the property. The doctor reflected a moment and asked, "Would $16,000 be too much?"

"You mean per acre?" asked Antonio.

The doctor shook his head. "No, I mean for the thirty acres." I looked at Doug, stunned.

The doctor must have thought we were crazy because we all started weeping. As was my custom, I didn't hesitate. "Yes! We'll take it!"

We all agreed the Lord had miraculously led us to the property, having already forged the way for us to buy that land.

Filled with unspeakable joy and amazement at God's work, I realized how much the Lord loves our praise. For the first time, I understood that He responds to our needs even while we praise Him. I had always known God loved our praise, but He proved it abundantly that day.

Praising Him made sense to me as I considered how I respond to praise from others and how my children and grandchildren respond when I praise them. As we express our love to God, He responds positively.

God knew our need for land before we'd asked Him. Expanding the Oaxaca area mission had been His plan all along. He had directed Antonio to the property and led me to the thorns that further opened my eyes and heart to His immense love and sacrifice for me and all humanity. Once again, He had shown us His desire to give more than we could ask or imagine (Ephesians 3:20). We had thought we needed three acres, but God wanted us to have thirty!

Thirty years have passed since I picked up that stem of thorns. I kept the branch, which has remained visible over my computer. I look at it often and remember the day a few brothers held hands in the middle of a field and praised our Lord and Savior, Jesus Christ.

I felt enthusiasm from that miraculous trip. Though we were short of funds to begin building, I knew God would provide. His work through

Medical Teams was abundantly clear. My job was to get the word out to people, and God would do the rest.

Medical Teams sent letters to donors, sharing our building plans and asking for their support, and we sought help from those who'd attended our banquets. Still, we came up short, but I believed the money would come.

Without the total funding, Antonio purchased the land, and we began construction by faith. We lived by faith, not sight (2 Corinthians 5:7). To the world, our actions indicated unwise business practices. Yet trusting in God had grown in our hearts with each experience of His divine presence, plans, and processes. At times, steps of faith make little business sense, but we must take steps in faith regardless.

Not everyone was on board. As we raised funds, Antonio's staff tested his faith. Convincing his team that the twenty-mile distance was the right location to build wasn't easy. He often heard discouraging feedback. Some staff didn't want to travel that far and back each day. Others said it was too far to be accessible to those in need. But Antonio reminded them that the Lord had chosen the location and that everything falls into place when God is in control.

We would find further financial support from an unlikely source.

In March 1990, God revealed a unique plan He was working on in Seattle, Washington. Local television and newspapers covered the following story reported in the *Seattle Times*. (It is my paraphrase.)

> A few months ago, Monte Clouston, 35, decided what his mission would be. He would build a house and sell it to help fund the construction of a hospital in one of Mexico's poorest regions, the state of Oaxaca, populated primarily by Indians.
>
> Clouston, a home builder, who also earned profits from apartment buildings he'd built, was experiencing burnout when he learned about Medical Teams' mission. He visited the impoverished area where volunteer doctors performed surgeries in a converted van.

"When you see a little girl who burned her hand in a fire—two of her little fingers burned down to the bones—and hiked two days for help . . ." Clouston knew he had to build the house to help the villagers. Many experiences among the Indians affirmed for Clouston that his mission was to help them—like seeing a beggar woman break into tears when she was given a leftover steak dinner from a restaurant.

He began making phone calls and writing letters. He would donate materials and find volunteers to help him build a spectacular three-bedroom, two-and-a-half-bath house. He plans to sell the new home and donate the profit to support the Oaxaca work of Medical Teams International.

The article motivated many people. Balser Investments donated a land lot; Parker Paints gave the paint; Hillsdale Pozzi came through with the doors; and on and on. Clouston hadn't needed to put much effort into selling his vision to suppliers, perhaps because he was passionate about it.

Individuals of diverse occupations donated time to the construction. Each helper gave their weeknights and weekends while working their day jobs to support their families.

He and his volunteers built the home, and Clouston sold it for $145,000 (1990 market value). Clouston donated the $80,000 profit (after costs) to the Oaxaca mission.

Monte gave unbelievable amounts of time to the house construction because he envisioned the healing and hope that a surgical clinic would bring countless villagers for years to come.

He and the volunteers had tremendous endurance and strong faith to complete the project. Monte later shared that what kept him going was concentrating on the rewards. "We had a mission and had to keep our focus on the result. We had to keep reminding ourselves what this project would accomplish in the lives of those Indians."

After the home-building project, Clouston took on another mission—on the property outside Oaxaca. He hosted a group of volunteers who spent two weeks with him there, helping to build the hospital. He said, "When I was down there, the things I saw moved me so much, I'll never be the same again."

Monte's commitment and endurance were amazing and motivating. I wanted more endurance so my tasks would not overwhelm me, and I wanted to stay the course at a strong, steady pace. I was committed to finishing the race I'd begun many years earlier. Through the grueling times, I was determined to win the prize—the crown Christ would hand me that couldn't tarnish and the words He'd say to me, "Well done, good and faithful servant" (Matthew 25:21).

Monte and his friends ran an incredible race and endured to the finish line. He is one of the finest examples of what an individual can do to form a team, raise funds and supplies, and see a taxing project to completion. He showed that we each could make a difference. Some talk and dream about helping, but Monte took action. The profit from selling the house made it possible to complete the surgical center, a school, a dormitory, and a dining hall! The thirty-acre campus was beautiful. We built two operating rooms where surgeons performed many more healing surgeries than before.

The new location did not deter people from coming. Though the staff had initially resisted the vision, they had trusted what Antonio told them. At the old clinic, they saw about thirty patients a day. On the first day at the new clinic, they treated the same number, and word of mouth quickly brought more in the days that followed. Before long, the staff was treating nearly two hundred people daily and even opened a dental clinic. To honor the dignity of those we served, we asked patients for a nominal fee but never turned anyone away.

Over the complex's lifespan, medical volunteers performed 25,000 surgeries and treated 250,000 people.

CHAPTER SIXTEEN

SUFFERING FOR GOD'S GLORY

I consider that our present sufferings are not worth
comparing with the glory that will be revealed in us.

— Romans 8:18

By 1992, our Mexico City mission, Manos de Ayuda, had increased beyond Antonio's ability to serve as the director while running the Oaxaca programs 350 miles south. The work was more than we could ask of one dedicated, hard-working man. We needed a director for the Oaxaca work.

Five years earlier (1987), Antonio had introduced me to a shy, quiet young man, Elias Betanzos, who was working as the accountant for our Mexico City office. Later, still serving as our accountant, he attended seminary, working toward ordination. We were glad to be providing employment that would help him become a pastor. He would later become ordained in the Church of the Nazarene. Around 1990, Elias moved to the State of Chiapas to pastor a church.

In 1992, when I'd asked Antonio to find a director for the Oaxaca mission, he said, "I have just the right person! Elias Betanzos." I was surprised.

"Antonio, I know Elias did a wonderful job for you in Mexico City, but are you sure he'll make an excellent leader? And isn't he pastoring a church in Chiapas?"

"Yes, Señor, he is. However, he also studied administration. He'll do an excellent job as the director. I'd like to ask him to consider the position." Antonio knew the quiet man better than I did, so I agreed.

Elias accepted and quickly took the initiative, demonstrating his decision-making authority. When Mexico was struck (several times) by overpowering hurricanes, Elias formed a medical team from his staff, organized relief supplies, and rallied help from individuals and churches. His example inspired many to give to those in need.

I was privileged to be present on an occasion when Elias shared his amazing and encouraging life story, which I had not heard before. I was astounded. The following is my paraphrase:

> I grew up in Chiapas, the southernmost state of Mexico bordering Guatemala, where most people live in extreme poverty.
>
> My father was a pastor. He was so poor he couldn't afford to buy shoes for his children. We often went to school barefoot and without breakfast. I vowed I would never live like that. I never wanted to be a pastor and be poor like my father. I studied administration because I didn't want to stay in Chiapas and risk poverty.
>
> I sought work in Mexico City. However, my father had committed my life to Jesus and believed God would use me. That was hard to imagine since I wanted no part in living a poor life.
>
> Nonetheless, I felt called to attend seminary while continuing work as an accountant at Manos de Ayuda. After I graduated, someone asked me to pastor a fledgling church in Mexico City. I fought the idea until I realized my family would remain financially secure from my job. I felt that accepting the pastorate would honor my father. The church was about 25 people but soon grew to about 250 people.

Receiving two salaries—one from the church and the other from Manos de Ayuda—I could afford to buy wonderful things for my family that I'd never thought possible. My future seemed secure from the poverty I'd experienced in my childhood. However, I would learn that God's ways are not our ways.

One day some people from Chiapas asked me to pastor their church of twenty-five elderly. They felt sure I was the man God wanted there, and I was sure I didn't want to be there. I promptly declined. I had two secure jobs supporting my family, so the move felt unwise. But inside my heart, turmoil began.

The Holy Spirit didn't let me rest, urging me to pastor the Chiapas church. I was distraught and asked God, "Why would You have me do this? I don't understand. I'm faithfully serving You at a church and the mission here. What more could You want?"

Still, I couldn't deny that He wanted me to go to Chiapas, and I desired to obey Him. His quiet voice won my heart. Although I didn't understand the purpose and the move seemed foolish, I accepted the pastorate and trusted that God had a bigger plan than I could fathom.

We moved to Chiapas into the church's small mud house, with creatures crawling all over the place. My family was courageous during those changes. I began the work I felt God wanted me to do, and soon the church grew to ninety people. Though the church was succeeding, my finances were dwindling. A year later, I was in the same state of poverty I'd worked hard to escape as an adult.

Antonio called and asked how I was doing. Not long into the conversation, I was in tears. I told him my daughter needed shoes, and when I'd gathered all my money, I found I had only thirty pesos [$3.50].

We had searched in town for shoes but didn't find a pair for that price. I thought of the times when my father had not been able to afford shoes for his children and the vow I'd made never to allow poverty to claim my life. With those thoughts, a rush of pain and embarrassment filled my soul, and I sat down on the curb and wept. I cried to God, "Why have you brought me to this place of poverty?"

Sometime later, several larger churches offered me positions, one near my wife's parents. We visited the church and accepted the job, hoping we'd rise above poverty.

As we traveled home to relinquish the Chiapas pastorate and pack what little we had, the Holy Spirit again convicted me. His quiet voice told me to decline the new position and continue with the church in Chiapas. His voice became so strong in my spirit that I called the other church, asked for their forgiveness, and declined the position.

Later when Antonio called with the offer to direct the work in Oaxaca, I knew better than to accept right away. Instead, I laid a fleece before the Lord and prayed. "Lord, I will take the position only if I'm also offered a pastorate for a church in Oaxaca."

In the meantime, I continued to serve the Chiapas church and community, and my poverty worsened. To provide for my family, I put up for sale the last vestige of my past—my old car.

When a group of four people approached our little mud home, I thought they were there to look at the car, and I began telling them about it. One interrupted and said, "We haven't come to buy your car. We're here to ask you to pastor our church in Oaxaca."

I couldn't believe it! I had never met the four people nor visited their church. They were, undeniably, God's answer to my fleece.

Elias and his family moved to Oaxaca, and he began work as director of Manos de Ayuda and pastor of a church of ten people. The church grew to be one of the largest Nazarene churches in the world, with over five thousand attending and seventy satellite churches reaching over twenty-five thousand people.

Also, the children's Bible Club of Manos de Ayuda, under Elias's leadership, grew from ten to twenty in one year. By 1999, over three thousand children attended weekly.

Pastor Elias was later elected president of an association of 2,100 Oaxaca churches of various denominations and appointed to the general board of the Church of the Nazarene worldwide. At this writing, he serves as superintendent of Mexico's Nazarene churches.

> To him who is able to do immeasurably more than all we ask or imagine, according to his power that is at work within us. — Ephesians 3:20

I'll always cherish Pastor Elias and the letter he wrote to me:

> There are three things I learned from you: your love for the poor, your integrity, and your generosity. I have tried to follow your example in those three areas, step by step. We continue helping the ones that are in need. I have tried to serve God with integrity, and I have been generous in my life. As a result, God has blessed our ministry.

What an amazing story of God's work! He called a young, quiet man who chose to humble himself before the Lord and used him to reach countless people.

As I reflected on Elias's journey, I understood why God had taken him from success to poverty. The church in Chiapas was Elias's wilderness, where God prepared and shaped him for the work in Oaxaca. Working for the Lord in poverty grew Elias's compassion for "the least of these."

Servanthood

> [God] called you out of darkness into his wonderful light. — 1 Peter 2:9

In Mexico, the government requires newly graduated doctors to perform two years of social medicine at a government clinic or nonprofit. Antonio requested the government to include our clinic among those who hosted young doctors. His petition was granted, and Dr. Maria de la Luz Portillo arrived at our clinic.

Typical of most graduate doctors, Maria wanted to hurry through her two-year requirement and move into private practice. However, as she worked for the clinic, her feelings changed. "Each day I saw poor people coming to me for help because they had no money. Yet out of gratitude, they offered a chicken or something else that may have been their last provision. They were so appreciative of what I'd done for them."

Each time I visited the clinic, I saw changes that had blossomed in Dr. Maria. Her compassion for the people increased, and her walk with God deepened. When she completed her term, she hesitated about what to do with her future and chose to continue working in the clinic. Antonio reminded her, "We can't pay you what you could earn if you went into private practice."

Maria paused in thought and then said, "I know you can't pay me much, but I cannot leave these people."

Considering the salaries of U.S. doctors, Dr. Maria's beginning salary at the clinic of $350 a month was strikingly meager. Yet she chose to continue serving the poor. She showered patients with her beautiful smile and compassion, demonstrating her love for the work and the people. What a joy to observe her listening carefully as elderly Indians explained their health problems and see her put her arms around many individuals to speak words of love. There are countless stories of her compassion and care.

The love and mercy Dr. Maria showed to the poorest of the poor continued for years at Manos de Ayuda, and she eventually became the medical director. Our teams loved her. Her name is so fitting, translated Maria of the light. She is a shining light of God.

After nine years with Manos de Ayuda, Maria faced another life-changing decision. One of our surgeons suggested she return to school to specialize in ophthalmology. Maria agreed and gained admittance to a Mexico university. Though we hated to see her go, we realized the training was an incredible opportunity for her. There were few ophthalmologists in Oaxaca. She had given years of service to her people and Medical Teams, and now she would pursue another love in health service.

Dr. Maria was getting ready to say goodbye to the clinic staff when she walked into Elias's office and said, "I cannot do it!"

"Why?" Elias asked.

"I believe God wants me to stay. I can be more helpful to our people here, doing what I'm doing." She withdrew from school and remained at Manos de Ayuda as medical director, forfeiting the salary and broader opportunities she would have had elsewhere.

Some may view such a decision as foolish, but God's will is always the wisest choice.

> It is God who works in you to will and to act in order to fulfill his good purpose.
> — Philippians 2:13

Dr. Maria, Elias, Antonio, and many other staff members and volunteers showed amazing dedication to their callings! Serving the Lord by serving the poor, they each discovered what it means to put others before themselves as Jesus had. He came to serve, not to be served (Matthew 20:28). If we love Christ, we are to feed His children (John 21:17).

I've often thought of the moment years earlier when I got up from listening to the evening news in my easy chair and followed Christ. That step led me to know and serve God with people like Antonio, Elias, and Maria. I've experienced God's wonderful love through them and countless others who serve Him by serving others. Such individuals share the same priority:

> "Love the Lord your God with all your heart . . . . 'Love your neighbor as yourself.'" — Mark 12:29–31

What a different world we'd have if more people lived this commandment.

CHAPTER SEVENTEEN

THE POWER OF TOUCH

Religion that God our Father accepts as pure and faultless
is this: to look after orphans and widows in their distress.

—James 1:27

"I knew I'd be punished if I showed her my report card without straight A's," explained the seventeen-year-old boy, describing in court why he had killed his mother with an axe.

Having endured extreme abuse since age four, the boy said he couldn't take it anymore. He added that his mother had never spoken words of love or even touched him. He killed her to escape her ongoing wrath.

Tragically, stories of child abuse are common. In our fast-paced culture, rampant with the pursuit of perfection, one vital element is often missing in children's lives: consistent encouragement and validation, whether pats on the back, kisses on the cheek, or sincere hugs and "I love you's."

When our children were young, their playing while Jean and I entertained friends would sometimes be disruptive. I'd become irritated and ask them to play elsewhere, so I understand the disciples' irritation in Mark 10:13–14:

> People were bringing little children to Jesus for him to place his hands on them, but the disciples rebuked them. When Jesus saw this, he was indignant. . . . "Let the little children come to me, and do not hinder them, for the kingdom of God belongs to such as these."

After Jesus admonished the disciples, He demonstrated something critically important:

"He took the children in his arms, placed his hands on them and blessed them" (Mark 10:16).

I can visualize Jesus bending down to the children's level, looking into each child's eyes, smiling, hugging each one, patting a rambunctious boy on the shoulder, and lightly touching the cheek of a shy girl. Jesus knew the importance of attention and touch to children. He knew we could never become the people He wanted us to become unless we received and shared attention and touch.

This truth was brought to my attention in 1990 while watching the news. Over one hundred thousand Romanian children—desperately ill, starved, abused, and neglected—were discovered in hundreds of ill-kept, state-run orphanages. I was shocked and grieved seeing their skeletal and deformed bodies and hearing the news anchor describe their horrific abuse and neglect.

In brief, Romania's former Communist dictator, Nicolae Ceausescu, banned contraception and mandated women have no less than five children. His goal was to build a special army in his quest to attain world power, just as Hitler had tried by developing the Hitler Youth organization.

With Romania's economy in shambles, families couldn't afford to raise multiple children. Many parents believed Ceausescu's lie that the government was able to take better care of their children than they could. The average Romanian worker earned about twenty-five dollars a month, not enough to feed a small family. Impoverished parents grievously turned their children over to the state. Most would never see them again, and none knew what their children would face.

A grading system determined where state workers sent each orphan. Those without physical and mental flaws were sent to newly-constructed buildings and stringently raised in Communist doctrine. Children with any physical or mental imperfections, including minor defects like cleft lip, club feet, and strabismus (crossed eyes), were deemed "irrecoverable" and sent to inhumane environments: converted buildings with no heat (winter temperatures dropped below freezing)

. . . little to no clothing . . . often naked and tied to their beds . . . lying and sitting for days in their waste in cribs with multiple children on torn and filthy mattresses.

Sexual and physical abuse were constants. Workers whipped children who cried or wet the bed. Food was grossly insufficient. Children slowly starved and contracted diseases, illnesses, and irreversible conditions caused by extreme malnutrition.

Many "irrecoverable" children had correctable physical problems, but 40 percent died yearly from gross neglect.

A crucial aspect of the orphans' physical, mental, and emotional decline and failure to thrive was that workers didn't hold, cuddle, kindly touch, or otherwise give any positive attention to them.

In the aftermath, the psychiatric and other science research communities pioneered the first studies on human physical touch and attention related to child development and the human brain. Studies showed that lack of human touch and attention by different degrees to children of various ages damage *every* aspect of human development. Many issues are irreversible—as evident in the extreme case of the Romanian children.

Research indicates that physical touch releases the brain chemical oxytocin, which "makes you feel more generous, more empathetic and nurturing, more collaborative, and more grateful—all of which help make you a good partner, parent, friend, and co-worker. Gratitude, in particular, is such a powerful bonding emotion that many scientists have deemed it the psychological 'glue' that keeps people close." [5] Gratitude and overall health are *impossible* without compassionate human touch, positive attention, and other developmental stimulation, demonstrated by Jesus's example of intermingling with children and the many scriptures about how to raise children.

Also, the orphans weren't allowed to play or have objects to focus on—a lifeless existence that immensely contributed to their acute underdevelopment, deformities, and lifespan decline. Rescuers found children of all ages rocking themselves back and forth, beating their heads against the cribs, and displaying other adverse behaviors now understood as directly related to touch and attention.

Faith In Action

Faith by itself, if it is not accompanied by action, is dead.
— James 2:17

When Medical Teams learned of the orphans' heinous circumstances, our board installed ministry teams in Romania. With prayer, we searched for ways to improve their lives. Our primary focus was caring for the "irrecoverable." A prime goal was to help the children's

5 Taylor Mallory Holland, "Facts About Touch: How Human Contact Affects Your Health and Relationships," April 28, 2018. *Dignity Health: https://www.dignityhealth.org/articles/facts-about-touch-how-human-contact-affects-your-health-and-relationships.*

likelihood of being placed in attentive orphanages with retrained staff for the opportunity of adoption. Achieving this meant recruiting specialty medical teams to perform corrective surgeries, hoping to eliminate any excuse that would keep the children institutionalized.

We sent our program director, Doug Rawlins, to assess the institutions. He found that everything needed to perform surgeries would require U.S. sourcing and shipping to Romania because of the orphanages' shortage of basic medical tools and equipment.

Once again, God arranged the transportation. The orphans' afflictions moved the heart of the senior vice president of Evergreen Airlines in McMinnville, Oregon. She helped by approaching the owner, Del Smith, on our behalf. He agreed to donate the use of a 727 airliner to transport our first medical team, equipment, and supplies to Romania.

After initial surgeries, some of the first adoptions of the children were by American families. Our hope was realized! Varied corrective surgeries freed many orphans. Medical Teams International became the number one agency worldwide for performing the most surgeries to help bring hope and a future of compassionate touch and attentive care to Romanian orphans.

Our mission was also to improve the living conditions of children who would remain orphans. Hundreds of our teams to Romania made needed repairs to the many orphanages. Our volunteers installed heating systems and laundry equipment; repaired showers; replaced toilets, sinks, faucets, broken windows, and damaged mattresses; and completed other improvements. We even built playgrounds.

Those remarkable teams also demonstrated their love in other ways, quickly building relationships with the children and simply extending love. Workers often left in tears. Having seen the difference their touch and attention made in the children's quality of life, many returned to Romania repeatedly to do more.

Our further concern was the orphans' mental stimulation. We developed a curriculum volunteers taught to orphanage staff to help stimulate babies' brains to develop normally. Teams of stimulation specialists went to Romania as trainers. Old ways don't change overnight, so the work required our volunteers to have great patience. We celebrated each child's various developments.

We learned that institutionalized children were released to the streets at age eighteen, lacking development in every regard and without training and skills to gain jobs or survive on their own. Consequently, many turned to prostitution, desperately craving human contact, and to street crime, seeing no other options. In the U.S. and around the globe, we see the same outcomes in many people who survived childhood abuse and neglect.

Since Communist Romania had been without the gospel for so long, the orphans knew nothing about our loving God and Jesus Christ. We asked orphanage directors if we could hold weekly children's Bible clubs. To our surprise, they granted permission!

Due to our years of experience starting Bible clubs in Mexico, we quickly and easily began the program in Romania. Each week, the orphans in our Bible clubs met with a Romanian Christian who extended love, touch, and attention; taught songs; and shared Scripture. The leader would read a Bible story, explain it, and seek to make the story relevant to the orphans' daily lives.

The Bible clubs reached thirteen orphanages with an average weekly participation of 1,500 children! Our club volunteers saw early on that the children's most vital need was physical touch. Simply holding them and caressing their arms or hands while speaking to them in loving tones evoked enormous responses. Groups of five or six children often surrounded and clung to our volunteers, yearning for more physical contact. As rotating volunteers prepared to return home, they wept, having established a special bond with the children.

The Romanian orphans should be a constant reminder of the vital importance of caring touch, attention, and encouragement. As parents and grandparents, we can learn from their developmental tragedies. Hug and hold children a little more and demand a little less.

> He took a little child whom he placed among them. Taking the child in his arms, he said to them, "Whoever welcomes one of these little children in my name welcomes me; and whoever welcomes me does not welcome me but the one who sent me." — Mark 9:36–37

My dad was not a hugger, but spending time with him later in life taught him to hug. Having my dad hug me, even though I was an adult, was wonderful. When I was a child, my mother's Saturday night custom was listening to the Grand Ole Opry on the radio from her rocking chair. I'd crawl onto her lap. She'd rock me as we listened together, and I'd fall asleep in her arms. After the show, she'd carry me to my bed.

Give lots of hugs to your children, grandchildren, nieces, and nephews, and hold the little ones. You'll be aiding their health and growth, building their sense of security and value, and storing splendid memories in them—dividends that pay for generations to come.

CHAPTER EIGHTEEN

EXTERMINATION

Love must be sincere. Hate what is
evil; cling to what is good.

— Romans 12:9

The door burst open and armed men rushed into her house, screaming orders to her father and brother to go outside. Frightened, nine-year-old Paymon grabbed her mother's hand as the men shoved them outside too. The Iraqi soldiers then herded her father and brother down the road with other captive men and boys forced from their homes. Terrified women and children ran after them.

Soon they reached the outskirts of the village, and the soldiers pushed the men and boys toward a field as they shouted orders. Paymon shook and cried with fear, holding tightly to her mother. "Mommy, why are they making them dig a hole?" She knew something bad was happening but was too young to realize what.

The captives were forced to dig a big trench. Then a soldier screamed at them to line up along it. Paymon cried out, "Don't hurt my papa!" Her cry would forever scream in her heart.

The soldiers aimed and fired at the men and boys. Paymon watched in terror as bullets ripped through her father and brother, spinning them around and into the trench. Horrified and grieved, she and her mother watched a bulldozer push the dirt onto the still-warm bodies.

Paymon would never forget that day. The images were seared permanently into her memory.

The atrocity was one of the hundreds playing out across Iraq in 1988.

A television personality had announced on Iraqi television that a wonderful day had come. "A gift from Allah. God is great!" he'd proclaimed. "God has given us permission to plunder the treacherous Kurds." (The Kurds are not Arabs but relate more to Europeans, though their predominant religion is Islam.)

The stories that followed the monstrous statement were barbaric. Saddam Hussein's army and secret police had unleashed a savage war on the Kurdish people in Northern Iraq.

When a dictator like Hussein declares "permission to plunder," he's giving his army and police license to also rape and massacre. His directive to "plunder" meant annihilating Kurdish Christians, Jews, and Muslims. The army and police plundered homes, raped women, shot the males, burned the crops, and wiped out nearly four thousand villages with poison gas.

Kurdistan was an independent nation covering an area of Iraq, Turkey, Syria, Iran, and Russia. After World War I, Britain and France divided the area for political reasons, and Kurds became the largest group in the world without a country, numbering over 22 million. They were a proud and productive nation, working the rich land of Northern Iraq's rolling hills and small mountains. They grew wheat and apples and raised large herds of cattle, goats, and sheep. Saddam was intent on crushing the Kurds and their economy, burning their wheat and apple orchards, stealing the herds they wanted, and killing the remaining livestock.

From 1988 to 1991, Saddam's army attacked the defenseless Kurds, killing them at will and forcing chosen men to join the army to strengthen Saddam's mission to destroy the nation. Can you imagine being forced to kill your own people?

In 1991, the Kurdish Rebel Army drove Saddam's forces out in the hope of restoring an autonomous state. However, the relentless leader reorganized his forces and returned with renewed vengeance. He sent his army with tanks, artillery, and brutal methods that caused the Kurds to flee into the freezing mountains along Turkey's border with only the clothes on their backs. Because Turkey had been at war for years against the Kurdish rebels, they wouldn't permit the fleeing Kurds into Turkey for safety. The people's only option was the mountains.

Even nature, it seemed, attempted to eradicate the Kurds. The extreme weather of the high snow-packed mountains took its toll on them. Every family lost children and their elderly to harsh climate exposure and starvation. Families buried their deceased babies by the hundreds.

Help came through the United Nations—the coalition forces that had fought against Saddam the previous year in the Gulf War. President Bush told the Iraqi Army to pull back or they'd be attacked, and sent forces to ensure the Iraqi Army retreated.

The UN dropped food, medicine, and tents to the Kurds. UN forces attempted to communicate with the people, telling them to come down from the mountains where more food, better shelter, and medical care awaited. International Rescue Committee and other aid organizations did a magnificent job overnight, constructing a city of camps with latrines—one of modern times' most extraordinary relief efforts to save such a large group of people. But the refugees were too frightened to leave the mountains.

Days passed as the UN tried to convince them of the camps' safety. At first, people trickled in, but suddenly, refugees appeared in droves—thousands of cold, sick, and hungry people staggering to safety.

Watching the televised scenes, I knew Medical Teams needed to reach out to the Kurds.

Restoring Hope

> You prepare a table before me in the presence of my enemies. — Psalm 23:5

The two enormous blades slowly rotated and picked up speed, causing the German Army transport helicopter to vibrate. It lifted straight up one thousand feet, hovered for several minutes, and then moved forward, picking up speed. We flew low, and I wondered why.

The man beside me leaned over and said, "Look out the window!" I gazed through the small pane and saw a U.S. Army helicopter gunship flying below, a hundred feet from our side. A man across the aisle said, "There's one on this side too." All doors on both sides of the gunships were open, and in each doorway stood a soldier ready to use his heavy machine gun. Then I understood. We were flying low with two escorts to protect us from ground fire.

I was traveling to meet the two medical teams we'd sent to Zakhu, Iraq. They were working against monumental challenges to save malnourished children and babies. Helicopters were the only way to get into the area. A group of television and newspaper reporters traveled with me to cover news of our mission endeavors. There were many needs.

To aid as many suffering people as possible, one of our teams ran a clinic in the vast, tented city built in a wheat field outside Zakhu. The other team worked in the mountains where thousands of Kurds remained, fearing Hussein's army.

As we flew into the mountains, I saw hundreds of tents. The refugees were camped along streams and valleys, living in horrendous conditions. Our military supplied clean drinking water and food by helicopter and set up a filtration system to produce clean water from the contaminated streams.

I arrived, and a British Army colonel overseeing the area walked me to the location of our medical team. As we walked, the ground suddenly shook with an enormous explosion. I almost dove to the ground but saw that the officer hadn't flinched. "What was that?" I asked.

"Oh, sorry about that. We just exploded more land mines," he explained. "Every day we search for land mines planted by Saddam's army and explode them." Tragically, despite best efforts, mines would continue to blow the Kurds apart for years.

Our team performed strenuous tasks behind military lines. Cholera, caused by drinking contaminated water, was a major concern. Cholera could kill within twenty-four hours, so our team set up separate tents to treat those patients more quickly.

There were also suffering people in Dohuk, a city thirty miles from the camp. To aid them would require our team to pass through Iraqi Army lines, hostile territory. International agencies serving the area met with UN representatives to determine a solution: UN officials would arrange a military convoy to travel to Dohuk with supplies and volunteers. The mission would be risky.

Other agencies in the area declined the risk, but our lead doctor, Travis Cavens, had offered to go.

When I discovered the special team had left for Dohuk, mixed emotions filled me. I wavered between concern for their safety and pride for their courage. Thankfully, UN forces led them there without incident, and our medical professionals began screening the sick and meeting the most urgent needs.

That night, Iraqi State agents slipped into the area and began firing weapons. The medical team was at their hotel and heard bullets hitting the outside walls. Since UN police had promised to protect them,

Dr. Cavens carefully watched for their arrival while witnessing the gunfire. When the shooting continued, he and the team retreated to the basement, hoping for greater safety, only to find the UN police hiding there!

The lack of police protection forced the team to abandon the mission. UN military escorted the group safely back to Zakhu.

Receiving Gratitude and Gaining Greater Responsibility

Overwhelmingly grateful for our military's presence and protection, and the presence and aid of relief agencies like Medical Teams, the Kurdish refugees repeatedly showered us with their affection. Whoever we passed would stop and wave. The men saluted us, and the children had learned to say in English, "Hello, mister," which they said to both males and females. We witnessed this phenomenon: where there is a true need and compassionate response, there are no religious or cultural barriers. Though the Kurds are Muslim, no aid had come from any Muslim country; all help had come from the Christian West. Jesus broke all barriers as He served others.

In June 1991, panic struck the Kurds in the valley, and they prepared to flee to the mountains again. Protecting military forces were leaving the region, but the refugees didn't know that some were staying to continue protecting them. UN officials hastened to explain that some military personnel would remain, and jet fighters would fly over the area daily to warn the Iraqi Army not to cross the line. The refugees were comforted. The planes were a sign of safety, convincing them to stay in the camp.

As the U.S. military prepared to pull forces from Northern Iraq, they requested that Medical Teams International take charge of the large medical warehouse distributing 90 percent of all medical relief supplies used during the expansive relief effort. The supplies represented millions of dollars. We agreed but didn't realize the enormity of the task. Our medical teams returned home, but other volunteers stayed to fulfill our commitment to manage the warehouse.

Over a year later, we were still managing the warehouse. We had distributed over $30 million in medical supplies and needed a coordinating director. We asked God to send someone. We would later learn He had already been at work on the answer.

Right Where He Wanted Them

> "By their fruit you will recognize them. Do people pick grapes from thornbushes, or figs from thistles? Likewise, every good tree bears good fruit." — Matthew 7:16–17

"I'm not certain what we can do, but let's do something," Mike Carson said to his wife, Mary, and his friend Bob Blincoe, who were part of Frontiers Mission.

The Carson and Blincoe families prepared to travel to Zakhu, Iraq, to help the Kurdish refugees. All members of the two families felt called to volunteer. In their hope of being allowed entry by the Iraqi government, they first traveled to Jordan and learned the Iraqi language, Arabic.

When the UN military first entered Northern Iraq with supplies, officials had discovered that an essential need was missing: translators. So, when Mike and Bob entered the scene, they were like Arabic-speaking angels sent from heaven. Sighing with relief, officials assigned the newcomers to register newly arriving refugees. As they worked among the people, they learned the Kurdish language.

These two families demonstrated Christ through good deeds rather than preaching about Jesus. They knew their calling to serve and awaited God's further instructions on how to carry out that mission.

Likewise, Medical Teams awaited God's answer for a director for the warehouse. The missing pieces were about to come together, perfectly fitting.

While on a trip to Zukhu, our program director met Bob Blincoe, who shared his goals. Our director recognized that Bob was our answer to prayer and asked him to consider serving as the warehouse director.

Bob discussed the role with Mike, and they both volunteered! I met the duo and agreed that the two men were more than qualified. Bob would serve as the director and Mike as his assistant. The two families were the only American families living in Northern Iraq.

Bob and Mike showed great insight into developing better ways of distribution to humanitarian agencies in the region and Kurdish hospitals. With the help of a USAID contract, Mike developed a computer system that linked Kurdish hospitals together. The system helped hospital employees know which health problems existed in various parts of the country and the locations of medicines.

Bob managed one of his first projects with a little humor. In the 1980s, Saddam's army confiscated all the mountain people's donkeys, which were the villagers' means of traveling and carrying supplies. In response, Bob started "Project Hee-Haw," using the slogan, MULES 'R' US. In one of his newsletters, he wrote, "When you need a thousand donkeys, and you gotta have 'em fast, who ya gonna call?"

The answer was the U.S. Office of Foreign Disaster Assistance (OFDA). They donated over 1,000 donkeys to remote mountain communities. Bob and Kurdish workers delivered 1,010 among the villages in need. Bob said, "The delivery was an event every community will remember."

The Blincoes' and Carsons' commitment was admirable. They endured hardships serving in Northern Iraq—the government hated any work that helped the Kurds, so the Iraqi Secret Police put a reward on Bob's and Mike's lives.

Day and night, the Kurdish Rebel Army guarded the two families. Still, the enemy managed to burglarize the Blincoes' house and wrote death threats on their living room wall. But the threats didn't deter the two families. They all felt they were right where God wanted them, and He protected them.

The groundwork of love and care for the Kurdish people laid by aid workers paved the way for Bob to gain certain privileges when Dohuk University asked him to teach a U.S. history class. He agreed with one condition: freedom to teach all history, which included the Christian foundation of our country. The university agreed. His history students sometimes visited him after class to inquire about Christianity and went to Mike's house to learn more.

When I traveled with Bob, people often yelled out greetings to him. When we were downtown, people approached and hugged him. Watching Bob love the people was a wonderful sight.

> Preach Christ always, and when necessary, use words. — St. Francis of Assisi

Bob, Mike, and their families served the people the way Christ had: by example. They reflected His love genuinely. Their love in action for our Kurdish brothers and sisters was a joy to see!

God and Wrigley's Chewing Gum

> "I tell you, if you have faith as small as a mustard seed, you can say to this mountain, 'Move from here to there,' and it will move. Nothing will be impossible for you." — Matthew 17:20–21

Bob and I were traveling in his utility van to the city of Mosul in Iraqi territory when we passed Dohuk—the Kurdish Rebel Army's outpost boundary between their people and the Iraqi Army's first checkpoint. Within two miles, we arrived at the checkpoint, and my heart beat faster as a lump formed in my throat. We were Americans in hostile territory, and our army had just defeated theirs. *How will they respond to us, their enemy?*

As we approached, I looked across the rolling hills of wheat. On every knoll, as far as the eye could see, sat a tank with its gun pointed north toward the Kurds, seeming ready to attack in force. *Lord, I ask for your protection.* Doubt rose in me about our decision to cross the Iraqi military line. This mission to further help the Kurdish people was no small endeavor. *Have we made the right decision?*

Private volunteer agencies lacking funds were planning to withdraw from Iraq. When I'd traveled to Dohuk, intending to close our operation, I saw the still compelling needs. Frigid winter months loomed, and the refugees continued living in tents without heat and with only a few blankets. The people would become sick in the harsh conditions. I knew Medical Teams had to stay. I promised Bob and the Kurdish workers that I would ask donors to continue the medical programs. Many donors responded to the enormous needs. I could not have foreseen that our Kurdish mission workers in Dohuk would grow to 150 and continue helping the refugees for another six years.

When I returned to Iraq in April 1992, an additional threat was hovering over the refugees like an ominous storm cloud. They no longer had the essential veterinary vaccines to protect their livestock. The animals were core to the people's livelihood. Their veterinarians had worked for the Iraqi government and had fled with their people. They lived among the displaced, unable to provide the needed veterinary medicines.

Due to the collapsed economy, livestock had become as crucial as money. Without medicines and vaccines to heal and protect cattle, goats, and sheep, their life source would die. Vaccines were the most immediate need—to prevent hoof-and-mouth, cattle fever, and other diseases such as parasites that had infected the sheep. Without vaccines, the livestock population was at risk of perishing.

Bob had sought help from the UN and the U.S. State Department but feared the animals would die before help arrived. He asked Medical Teams (the largest agency serving in Northern Iraq) if we could help in the meantime, and we did.

Bob purchased a vaccine from Europe, but the lengthy arrival time threatened the hope of saving the livestock. In his search for alternative resources, he learned that a Kurdish man in the nearby city of Mosul, behind enemy lines, had access to the vaccine. Ironically, he could get the vaccine from the Iraqi government without them knowing where the medicine would go. He'd said he would risk his life to get the vaccine to save his people's livestock.

Bob, concerned for the man's safety, planned to help by traveling the forty miles into Mosul to meet him covertly and pick up the vaccine. A dangerous endeavor. Saddam had placed an in-country embargo on anything going north to the Kurds. Soldiers at checkpoints searched all vehicles and confiscated whatever could benefit the Kurdish. Military officials often pulled cars over and drained the diesel, leaving only enough for the travelers to reach their destinations. They burned the drained fuel on the side of the road.

I was deeply concerned for Bob's safety, knowing the military would never allow vaccines to reach the Kurdish. He had shared, "I'll have to pass through three or four checkpoints each way."

"Isn't that dangerous?" I stressed.

"Yes, but I'll say I'm with the United Nations. I'm at less risk than the Kurdish man. If Iraqi soldiers discover him traveling with a vaccine to help the Kurdish, they'll execute him. If he's willing to risk his life, surely I can try to help."

"Who are you taking with you?"

"I won't allow anyone to accompany me." And I could not allow Bob to go alone.

"I'm going with you," I said firmly.

"Ron, I have papers that allow me to be here," he argued. He reminded me, "You came into Iraq through the back door with no visa to be in Iraq." Medical Teams and others had entered through Turkey because the Iraqi government would not grant visas to aid workers. Bob had gotten his visa before the war. Still, I could not let Bob take the risk alone. I would suffer far more if I were not by his side to help him if something went wrong. I insisted, and Bob finally agreed.

As we approached that first checkpoint, my anxiety grew. A military police officer motioned us to stop. He asked, "Who are you?"

Bob explained, "We're Americans on our way to Mosul." Hearing "Americans," the soldier smiled, and Bob casually continued. "We're working with the United Nations and need supplies." The officer waved us through.

Later, thinking of the soldier's smile reminded me that the soldiers were not our enemies. We fought against corrupt governments, dictators, and generals that held the Iraqi Army accountable.

After years of traveling to former Communist countries like Russia, whose people I once believed were my enemies, I realized they were people like me who loved their families and simply wanted to work and live in peace.

We seamlessly passed through the next two checkpoints and arrived in Mosul that afternoon. We explored the city, waiting for the cover of darkness to get the vaccines, which were stored at a safe house.

Sidebar: Centuries ago, Mosul had been the ancient city of Nineveh that Jonah had walked into and conveyed God's message: they had forty days to repent, or He would destroy them (2 Kings 14:25; Jonah 3).

Jonah's journey was arduous—he weathered a terrific ocean tempest and survived three days in the belly of a great fish that then vomited him onto land. From there, he traveled over 150 miles inland on foot, a three-day journey into hostile Ninevite territory, obeying God (Jonah 1–3).

Also noteworthy, Mosul is at the center of the Islamic State (IS) that took over the city in 2014, murdering thousands of people. The IS was finally defeated in 2018 when Iraqi, Kurdish, and American forces drove them out.

As Bob and I drove around the city, passing the time until nightfall, we saw remnants of old walls and gates of ancient Nineveh. I imagined the Ninevite king listening to Jonah's message. The king had fallen to the ground, torn his clothes in repentance, and declared a fast. He and the people sought God's forgiveness and turned from their evil ways (Jonah 3).

Their remorse must have given way to great joy when they experienced God's compassion, mercy, and forgiveness. When I reflect on God's great love and forgiveness, I feel the warmth of His grace.

Bob and I marveled at the sunset, followed by the purple brilliance of twilight twinkling over Mosul. Then we drove to the safe house.

When we arrived, I told Bob, "I'll stay in the van. I don't want to take the chance that the secret police will make me identify the man with the vaccine. I'll look straight ahead while you retrieve the boxes and put them in the van."

Moments later, when I heard Bob close the van's back doors, I looked behind me. The entire rear was filled with boxes to the ceiling, visible through the backdoor windows. When Bob climbed into the driver's seat, I asked, incredulous, "How are we going to pass through the checkpoints with so many boxes? The police will see them at the first checkpoint!" Fear had seized my heart. "There's no way we can hide that many boxes."

Bob was stoic and committed. "I know, but we must try."

Immediately, I recalled the story of Brother Andrew, known as "God's smuggler." During the Cold War, Bibles were illegal to own in Communist Russia and to import into the country. Brother Andrew repeatedly smuggled in Bibles. He'd pack them in suitcases, pray that God would blind the eyes of the agents, and take the cases through customs. Miraculously, he always passed through without incident. He was known for having smuggled thousands of Bibles into Russia.

I reminded Bob of God's smuggler. Then I asked him to pray with me. "Lord, the Kurdish need this vaccine. Will you blind the eyes of the police at the checkpoints, so they won't see what we have? We ask this in the name of Jesus."

Bob started the van, and we drove north.

At the first checkpoint, the guard waved us through. Our hearts pounded as we continued driving, whispering thanks to God.

At the next checkpoint, my faith soared when the guard waved us through. God was protecting us.

A mile from the final checkpoint, I could see the lights of Dohuk in the distance, which felt like home, representing safety. Near the checkpoint stood concrete barriers, forcing vehicles to slow and preventing drivers from speeding past. Also ahead was the fiery light of burning diesel along the roadside. Black smoke rose slowly like a snake about to strike. The image felt like a bad omen, and I sensed that this checkpoint would be different. I felt weak as various evil scenarios slithered into my thoughts as if I were watching a horror film. I was in the country illegally and surrounded by guards taught to hate my people and those we were there to aid. I'd never felt so far away from my beloved country and family.

We stopped at the guardhouse, and a man in civilian clothes stepped out. He looked as though he hadn't shaved in three days and wouldn't be a fan. Bob whispered, "Secret Police." I'd heard of the atrocities they committed. They were dangerous.

The man harshly barked questions. "Who are you? Where have you been?"

Bob responded quietly, but the man's face didn't soften. His features seemed to rage with a desire to harm us. I figured his next question would be, "Where are your papers?" Two Americans had been imprisoned just days before for attempting to enter the country without papers. If he asked for my papers, prison awaited me.

Thankfully, the officer didn't ask, but his eyes drew to the back of our van. My heart thudded as I silently shouted, *He'll see the boxes!*

As he turned toward the back of the van, Bob grabbed a package of Wrigley's chewing gum from the dash and thrust the packet out the window, stopping the officer in his tracks. Bob asked him, "Do you like gum?"

The officer looked at the pack and then at the back of the van, back and forth several times. Seconds dragged by as he seemed to wrestle with a decision. When it looked as if he would continue to the back of the van, he suddenly turned, grabbed the gum from Bob's hand, and said in a gruff voice of dismissal, "Get out of here!"

My heart pounded as we drove on. "How did you know to reach for the gum?" I heaved to Bob. "And so quickly?"

"I don't know," Bob shook his head in wonder. "I grabbed it without even thinking."

We marveled over God's protection and divine creativity and safely reached Dohuk with the vaccine.

Bob hired Kurdish veterinarians and assistants to vaccinate thousands of animals, saving them and reestablishing the people's ability to earn income. The circumstance caused USAID to realize the great need for more vaccines. In response, they provided an enormous grant that enabled us to buy large quantities and hire more workers for the program. Soon the veterinarians were vaccinating twenty thousand animals a day.

Sharp and innovative, Bob devised a very efficient vaccination method that squeezed the value from every dollar. USAID told us the typical overhead cost for a single animal vaccination averaged twenty-two cents. Bob was purchasing the vaccine for nine cents! The program enabled the immunization of three million animals a year for four years, saving the entire animal herd of Northern Iraq. The animal population rose, and people once again had safe meat and income.

Bob wrote in his newsletter,

> The Kurds face many crises—enemies around and enemies within, water shortages, and no electricity—but the livestock vaccination campaign avoided one crisis. The work of providing cold vaccines has prevented famine and restored a portion of the trade economy to the Kurdish people of Northern Iraq.

"Before they call I will answer; while they are still speaking I will hear."
— Isaiah 65:24

The Kurdish would not forget the efforts of this mission. As Bob worked among the Kurds, he heard everywhere, "God bless America!"

Bob and I will never forget how God answered our prayers on the dangerous mission to and from Mosul. Our experience was heart-pounding, but God was in control. Whether He had blinded the eyes of the checkpoint agents or moved Bob to reach for the chewing gum, He had a plan to get the livestock vaccine to the Kurdish, and He protected us. The experience allowed us to see the Lord at work, and I realized something new about God. Wrigley's chewing gum? God has a profound sense of humor.

CHAPTER NINETEEN

COURAGE IN HELL

Who shall separate us from the love of Christ?
Shall trouble or hardship or persecution or
famine or nakedness or danger or sword?

— Romans 8:35

"We're placing premature babies who should be in incubators into cardboard biscuit boxes on the ground!" declared one of our seasoned volunteer doctors, Travis Cavens. Among the highly-skilled team were also Dr. Earl Van Volkinburg and exceptional nurses and paramedics. They were rendering lifesaving aid in the refugee camps of Goma, the Congo (DRC), working in a far more overwhelming, chaotic, and primitive situation than they'd faced before.

We had sent that particular volunteer medical team, the best, to Goma because the horrendous situation demanded hardy, skilled workers. They had previously served in other terrible conditions—the Cambodian camps, Ethiopia, Sudan, and Somalia—but the expert team encountered even greater despair and challenges in Goma. Upon seeing the people's devastation, a doctor said, "This is what hell must be like."

Dr. Cavens, in reflection, replied, "This is worse than hell."

The Hutu ethnic group had butchered over 500 thousand Tutsi-ethnic people in Rwanda in 1994. Eventually, the Tutsi Rebel Army defeated the Hutu army and took power. In fear of reprisals, the Hutus fled the country. The UN reported that 2.5 million had fled to surrounding countries, and another 2.5 million had fled and become displaced within Rwanda. Of the 2.5 million who fled the country, 1.2 million ended up in Goma, the Congo, with thousands dying before reaching the Congo. Of the 1.2 million camped along Goma's volcanic rock region, thousands died of cholera and dysentery from drinking contaminated water. The terrible suffering and the quickly mounting death toll prompted Medical Teams to send teams to a field hospital among four hundred thousand of the over 1 million refugees.

Before we traveled to Goma, UN officials briefed us about the situation. A few remaining Hutu Army soldiers still camped among the civilians, and the UN feared there could be shooting and rioting in the camp. They warned that the UN would have difficulty reaching us if we encountered trouble.

My heart was uneasy after I had learned we could not count on the UN's help. Some agencies weren't going to the camp for fear of being caught in gunfire.

Duly informed and focusing on our purpose—saving lives and trusting in God—our seasoned team agreed to work in the camp. As a precaution after arriving, I visited the U.S. military group serving in Goma and shared with an officer that Medical Teams, "fellow Americans," were working in the camp. Concerned for their safety, I said, "If we need help, I hope the cavalry will come."

The officer laughed and said, "Sir, we will do our best to come to your aid if needed." His reply gave me some comfort.

Upon first entering Goma, we'd driven about two miles when we encountered a wall of people blocking the road. We gingerly pushed through, taking forty minutes to travel four miles.

Entering the camp, we witnessed the devastating effects of four hundred thousand people camped on volcanic rock terrain that prevented digging latrines. The smell of human waste was overpowering. Everywhere we walked, we stepped in urine and feces.

The people's faces bore grief and defeat. Despite the vast number of people, an eerie silence hung over the vast camp.

Thousands of small huts made of branches congested the rock landscape. Our seasoned volunteers had never experienced such squalor.

The field hospital consisted of a few tents. Each was crammed inside with about a hundred patients. Nurses and doctors barely had room to walk. The tents also served as an outpatient hospital, treating hundreds daily.

Our team evaluated the hospital and supplies and saw the critical need for more tents, medicine, and food. The significant needs in the middle of nowhere triggered a sinking feeling in our volunteers. They prayed they could get by until a shipment arrived.

In the meantime, necessity inspired creativity, like foraging around the camp for helpful items such as medicines that other onsite agencies might be willing to give or trade for something they needed. Dennis Bean, one of our paramedics, took that task. As I'd seen many times before, Dennis, Nurse Erda Fuller, and other medical volunteers organized themselves and got busy saving lives.

The team admitted the sickest patients first and began IV fluids and antibiotics. Those patients would be monitored for a few days while Dr. Cavens and Dr. Van Volkinburg worked to treat the hundreds of outpatients who lined up outside each day for examinations and treatments.

Compassion

> When Jesus landed and saw a large crowd, he had
> compassion on them and healed their sick.
> — Matthew 14:14

"Bring me a spinal tap needle!" Dr. Travis Cavens shouted. "She may have spinal meningitis."

A nurse ran to the supply tent as he prepared the ten-year-old Rwandan girl for the test. The exam table was a board laid atop two sawhorses outside the clinic tent.

The exam confirmed spinal meningitis. "I'm not sure she'll be alive tomorrow," Dr. Cavens said as he put an IV in the child's limp arm to administer medicine that would fight the infection. She was unconscious and burning up with a fever.

Dennis was standing by, watching with concern. Dr. Cavens said to him, "Please be careful with the IV when you take her to a tent." Dennis gingerly picked up the motionless child and carried her to a cot.

The line of mothers outside, holding their babies and young children, felt almost overwhelming. There must have been 150 mothers waiting for our only pediatrician. *How can one doctor examine all these children?* I wondered what Dr. Cavens was thinking as he viewed the extensive line. He cared for them one at a time, as he had at other disaster sites. He and his assistants showed concern and compassion to each mother and child examined.

I was bunking with Dr. Cavens. That night, as we sat on our bunks reflecting, I asked him, "Do you realize how many children you examined today?"

"I have no idea," he responded wearily.

"Travis, you saw 217! That's an amazing accomplishment. They're all extremely sick." By comparison, he might see 30 children in a workday at his Longview, Washington, clinic.

He began to weep as I'd never seen before. Deep sobs gushed from his broken heart. I placed my hand on his knee. When he regained composure, he explained. "I'm crying for the sick children I saw today who might not be alive in the morning. I'm crying for the 130 still waiting in line when we had to leave." The UN required that foreign agency workers leave the camp at a specific time each night. Though the team didn't want to go, they needed the rest.

Dr. Cavens was running a race to save lives. Though he won many battles, he lost some. At such times, remaining positive was hard. Only strong hearts could manage what our team members experienced.

The following morning, I was overjoyed watching the volunteers' faces as they found improved patients. One who had been near death the day before was sitting up and taking food. Often I felt as though I were witnessing Lazarus-like resurrections, life returning where death had reigned.

For Dr. Cavens, the day was not joyous. The child with spinal meningitis had died. The grief was overwhelming as workers carried her small, lifeless body from the tent. Nurse Erda Fuller sobbed, "It isn't fair! It isn't fair!" Dennis put his arms around her, sharing the grief. Losing a child was always hard. We could only commit them into the arms of our loving God and embrace the confidence that they would never again suffer pain and hunger.

In August 2021, Dr. Travis Cavens exchanged his stethoscope for a heavenly crown from our Lord Jesus Christ, the One he loved and served. Our beloved brother and friend was a great encourager to Jean and me during our many years with Medical Teams. He had always been ready with a word of encouragement, inspiring us to do greater deeds.

The two most important things we can do in this life are to believe in the Lord Jesus Christ, which means loving Him with all our heart, mind, and soul; and to love our neighbor, which includes caring for the poor, the widows, and orphans. Dr. Cavens completed his earthly assignment. We're certain he heard the greatest words a person could ever hear: "Well done, my good and faithful servant" (Matthew 25:21 NLT).

Burial Preparations"

> Going to Pilate, he asked for Jesus' body. Then he took it down, wrapped it in linen cloth and placed it in a tomb cut in the rock, one in which no one had yet been laid. — Luke 23:52–53

Because I'm confident that heaven exists and is a wonderful place, at one time I wondered why we grieve the death of others. Now I realize we grieve the loss of relationships and the deep losses others feel. Losing my beloved parents, I knew they were safe with the Lord, yet I felt profound grief, knowing I would never talk with them or see them again for the rest of my earthly life. As I contemplate years in ministry among the grieving, many sad scenes come to mind. Groups of mothers in disbelief and despair, rocking back and forth as they sob over their lost children. As a father, my heart rips apart when I see other fathers grieving. I'll never forget the young Ethiopian father's reaction when told his son had died. He sat on the ground, folded his arms over his head, and tried hard not to cry, but his pain was too much to contain. He wept as he rocked back and forth, his face begging, *Please, not my son!* I wept for him. Though his son was safe in the arms of God, the precious dad would bear the weight of his loss for the remainder of his life.

At the Goma camp, there were no funerals, no proper burials, and the people didn't even know their loved one's burial place. As we drove to camp each day, we saw refugees stacking along the roadside the wrapped bodies of those who had died in the night. I learned that aid workers would come and collect the bodies for mass burial.

In my early days at the camp, seeing the newly laid bodies day after day, I wondered who had wrapped them in matting, carried them from camp, and placed them along the roadside. The answer swept over me in stark and crushing realization: *their loved ones!*

I imagined a father, mother, sister, brother, or friend lovingly rolling their departed loved one in matting while sobbing with grief and carrying their beloved to the roadside to be hauled away. Horrid.

I tried to put myself in the grieving refugees' place. *Could I roll in matting my deceased family members—my wife, Jean; our son, Bill; our daughters, Sheri and Dawn; our grandchildren, Kai, Halle, Sarah, Hope, Hannah, and Joshua? Could I place them along a roadway and walk away, knowing that strangers would haul them off and bury them in a mass grave somewhere unknown to me?*

My heart was so heavy as I pictured each of my family members. Words cannot describe such tragedy the refugees suffered. As I wept for them, my grief renewed my calling to do all we could to help relieve the people's suffering. God would have us do no less.

Good Samaritans

> "A Samaritan, as he traveled, came where the man was; and when he saw him, he took pity on him. He went to him and bandaged his wounds, pouring on oil and wine." — Luke 10:33–34

The sea of sick and starving people, their faces distraught, reminded me of the Bible's good Samaritan story. Jesus praised the one man who had stopped to help a stranger after others had passed him without stopping. The refugees' suffering fueled our volunteers' desire to be good Samaritans.

We set up a tent clinic along the road and stationed team members to give care there while other members continued work at the camp hospital clinic. We selected the tent site with help from local nationals. Before placing the tent, we spent considerable time clearing human waste from the area. The smell was overpowering. I was helping, and a paramedic yelled, "Watch out, Ron, you're about to step in it!" Laughter followed, much welcomed amid all the tragedy around us. Yet the teasing also caused me to consider further the refugees' dire situation: *These people have no privacy when they need to relieve their body waste!* The volcanic rock was not penetrable to install latrines. The locale had stripped the people of their dignity. Although our team had buckets in a makeshift toilet during our workday hours in the camp, my thoughts were on the refugees' displaced and bare lifestyle. Imagine four hundred thousand people without a single latrine!

While the team was organizing the tent set-up and supplies, refugees were already lining up for medical help. Within moments of completing final preparations, the line had grown to hundreds. The number of people and needs was so staggering that our team kept reminding themselves that they could help only one person at a time and were doing their best.

The first family that day was carrying the father on a stretcher. Our doctor had the painful task of telling them their loved one had died. Such a beginning did not appear promising to the team. Because of the additional clinic, our medical professionals did, however, save many more lives. Our volunteers truly functioned as good Samaritans. Their attentive care for each patient conveyed that the individual was valued and loved.

An elderly lady collapsed outside the tent. A nurse rushed to her side and cared for her. In one hand, the nurse held an IV bottle administering the lifesaving solution while stroking the lady's head with the other hand. I will always treasure that picture in my memory. The woman lived.

Wandering around the tent area, I made an exciting discovery. Next to the road was a hole in the igneous rock terrain. The opening was about three by five feet. I squatted low and peered in, finding an enormous cavern—a volcanic blowhole. Unable to contain my excitement, I shouted, "We can build a latrine!"

I asked a volunteer national to search for carpenters among the people walking the road. Moments later, the volunteer returned with several candidates. I told the men I'd pay them to collect wood and build a two-hole latrine. They agreed, and we had the first outhouse within three hours!

Deep satisfaction spread through me, and I chuckled, having never imagined I'd be so enthusiastic about an outhouse!

CHAPTER TWENTY

THE SOVIET UNION

The Lord is close to the brokenhearted and
saves those who are crushed in spirit.

— Psalm 34:18

A magnitude 6.9 earthquake leveled two major Soviet Armenian cities on December 7, 1988, killing 25,000, injuring 15,000, and making 517,000 homeless.[6] Leninakan was nearly destroyed, and Spitka had not one building left standing. The region's estimated death toll was up to 50,000.[7]

In response, Medical Teams organized an orthopedic surgery team to care for victims who'd suffered fractures. We learned that Armenian hospitals had few supplies and sparse medical equipment, so we hoped to fill those needs as well.

Once again, we were without transportation for our team and donated supplies. Flying Tigers Airline stepped up and donated a 747.

---

6 "December 1988 Leninakan-Spitak-Kirovakan, Armenia Images." *National Centers for Environmental Information: https://www.ncei.noaa.gov/access/metadata/landing-page/bin/iso?id=gov. noaa.ngdc.mgg.photos:10.*

7 "Data curbs earthquake risk in Armenia," February 16, 2016. *UNDRR: https://www.undrr.org/ news/data-curbs-earthquake-risk-armenia.*

Our efforts in Armenia accomplished several "firsts," including the first American team ever granted entrance into the Soviet Union without visas, the first American medical team to work in Soviet Armenia, and the first Boeing 747 to land in that part of the Soviet Union. The landing was a significant event for those on and off the aircraft. Onlookers had lined the runway to watch the huge plane taxi in.

We learned that none of the gangplanks could reach the door of an aircraft that large, so we deboarded by climbing down a ladder. Unloading the cargo was done manually because the airport had no equipment, and transporting the supplies to the hospital required fifteen military trucks. Once the trucks were loaded, we climbed on provided buses and convoyed with the trucks to the hospital in the capital of Yerevan, where we'd work.

My precious wife, Jean, accompanied me, and we experienced something grand. We were working with Dr. Jerry Becker in a tent in the hospital's parking lot when I heard a car drive up. Curious, I stepped out and almost bumped into the visitor—Mother Teresa! She had arrived to visit the hospital.

What a grand privilege it was for me to spend five minutes alone with the incredible woman. She was tiny—just a little taller than my waist—and appeared frail. But her face glowed with a radiance that could only have been the love of Christ. When I tried to praise her incredible work, she drew her hands together in prayer fashion and said, "Glory to God."

Jean then met her, and someone took a picture as Mother Teresa kissed a medallion and gave it to her. Forever after, Jean treasured the experience, medallion, and picture.

Pondering Mother Teresa's choice to live among the poor brought to mind a popular bumper sticker: "He who dies with the most toys wins." If that's true, Mother Teresa was a loser. Her earthly possessions had been few, as reported by the *Vatican Post* after her death: three saris, two or three habits, a girdle, a pair of sandals, a crucifix, a rosary, a plate, a set of cutlery, a cloth napkin, a canvas bag, and a prayer book.[8]

No possessions we have on earth will enter heaven. Mother Teresa's heavenly riches are far greater than this world could ever give or hold—everlasting rewards from God for her sixty years of love, compassion, kindness, and care bestowed on the poor.

> Whoever is kind to the poor lends to the Lord,
> and he will reward them for what he has done.
> — Proverbs 19:17

A reporter once asked Mother Teresa, "You take kids off the streets of Calcutta who are ill or frightened, and some of them die. Would you say your work is successful?" She answered, "God has not called me to be successful. God has called me to be faithful."

I shared with Mother Teresa that I had read the quote years earlier and had worked to build our mission on her words. Because I'm a go-getter who wants to get things done yesterday, I've had to remind myself to be faithful to God, those we serve, and those who make our worldwide missions possible. As I write this, Medical Teams International is still faithfully serving the needy forty-one years later. They continue to model the love of Jesus. I believe the team members, other volunteers, and donors know that their faithfulness is the ultimate in true success.

The earthquake aftermath was heartbreaking. Our surgical team encountered people with broken bones and no pain medicine lying on carts in hallways, waiting for care.

Jean made rounds with our doctor one morning and followed him into a room where he examined a woman's ghastly open wound to her foot. The dressing needed to be changed, and there was no means to

---

8 "3 Things We Can Learn From the Life of Mother Teresa," Augusts 16, 2016. *Vatican Post: https://www. vaticanpost.com/3-things-can-learn-life-mother-teresa/.*

alleviate her pain. He carefully redressed the injury, and she thanked him and then grabbed his hand and shook it. Then she motioned Jean closer. Jean extended her hand, thinking the woman wanted to shake hands, but she grasped Jean's hand and pulled her close, tears coursing down her cheeks. She kissed the back of Jean's hand and up her arm in an outpouring of gratitude. They wept together, both overcome with emotions as Jean knelt beside the small bed, her arms wrapped around the woman. Then she leaned over and kissed the woman's forehead.

Jean later shared the story with me and said, "I believe our teams did more for human relations than all the politicians put together." I agreed. Christ's love overflows every political division and unifies humanity, disregarding race, religion, and birthplace so all people are neighbors.

> "Love one another. As I have loved you, so you must love one another." — John 13:34

I faced an embarrassing situation in the hospital. Our team was assigned lodging in patient rooms, and Jean and I shared a room. When I went into the bathroom to shower, I was shocked to find an enormous bare window exposing the shower! There I was, on display to all who passed outside. That was the quickest shower I've ever taken. I rejoiced when the window fogged up.

The exposure later reminded me that we're all bare before God. Where can we hide from Him? Nowhere. Where can we hide our thoughts from our Creator? Nowhere. Where can we hide our secret actions from Christ? Nowhere.

> Nothing in all creation is hidden from God's sight. Everything is uncovered and laid bare before the eyes of him to whom we must give account. — Hebrews 4:13

Before I was born, God knew me, designed me, and knitted me together in my mother's womb. I was born naked. Who among us feels we can ever hide ourselves or our sins from God? There is no place, not even a cave or under a rock. We're always visible to our Creator, and we will one day stand before Him and give an account of our earthly lives. I invite you to pray with me:

> Search me, God, and know my heart; test me and know my anxious thoughts. See if there is any offensive way in me, and lead me in the way everlasting. — Psalm 139:23

CHAPTER TWENTY-ONE

WHY, LORD?

"I will have mercy on whom I have mercy, and I will
have compassion on who I have compassion."

— Romans 9:15

Somali refugees poured across the border into Kenya in 1993. Famine and war ravaged their country, and over 250 thousand fled the horrors. Unwelcomed in Kenya, the displaced people ended up encamped outside Wajir, Kenya. Medical Teams traveled there to aid them.

Wajir had the appearance of the last stop on the way to nowhere. Someone said, "Wajir is not the last place on earth, but you can see it from there." The streets were dirt, reminding us of old western movies that depicted America as a vast frontier dotted with dusty little towns. The people were poor, carving out a living by farming and raising livestock.

Our team included Dr. Dan MacDougall, a pediatrician, and his wife, Dr. Lindsay MacDougall, a pathologist. Dr. Lindsay set up an excellent laboratory for blood and urine testing, as no other laboratory existed. Because of her work, doctors more quickly and accurately diagnosed illnesses.

About fifty miles from camp was a large group of sick people living in the bush, and Dr. Dan wanted to take a small medical team to treat them. Local officials told us that travel was dangerous because bandits roamed the area. Despite their warnings, we attempted the mission, escorted by four armed local police.

We left early in the morning in two four-wheel drive vehicles. I drove the lead vehicle, and one of our national workers directed me. The police had told me, "Drive fast and do not stop," a ploy to lessen bandits' ability to overtake us. However, the road was soft dirt, so we could move only at about forty-five miles an hour and frequently had to slow to avoid hitting camels, giraffes, and donkeys.

After about forty miles, with no signs of civilization, I was surprised to see a man shuffling toward us on foot. *Where is he going? There's no destination out here—there's nothing.* The day was hot, and I pitied him. As we passed, my eyes met his. He was weak and had trouble walking.

Many thoughts came to my mind as our wheels rolled another five hundred feet. I thought of the good Samaritan parable and weighed the risks of stopping to help the man. *A stop will subject us to bandits and put us behind schedule. Hundreds of people are waiting for help. He's just one man.*

Suddenly, I felt compelled to stop, discarding risks and time. I stopped abruptly, jumped out of the vehicle, and asked Dr. Dan to examine the man. He motioned for a translator as our police escorts jumped out and began setting up a secure perimeter.

As we approached the man, he slumped to the ground. Dr. Dan diagnosed him as infected with malaria. Dan gave him water and the medicine he needed to get well.

Knowing we had done the right thing felt good, and God had protected us. Once again, I thought of the good Samaritan story: travelers who had passed the beaten man had somewhere important to go, as we did. Yet God had always impressed in me the importance of stopping for one. He assured me there would be a way to accomplish all the work He laid out for us, even if we stopped for one.

We arrived safely at the small village of Tarbaj and set up a clinic under an acacia tree. The medical team positioned stools in a circle to designate a treatment area. Word went out about the medical team's arrival, and within minutes, there was a line of people to be examined. They were so eager to get into the circle that our police escorts had to control the crowd.

A frequent medical problem was infection from thorns. Long, thorny bushes were everywhere, and stepping on one pushed a thorn deep into the foot. Dr. Allen Henderson surmised there were also sick people unable to walk to the clinic. He was right. Because of his insight, immobile people received medical attention in their huts. Dr. Henderson treated a woman whose foot was so infected and swollen that she couldn't walk. Had our team not reached her in time, she could have lost her foot to amputation or her life to infection.

Beneath the acacia tree marking the clinic site, Nurse Mary Sue Richards asked me to help retrieve a thorn from a young boy's swollen, infected foot. She probed the foot with a needle and said, "Ron, there it is. Grab it with your fingers and pull it out." I did, and as it emerged, I was amazed to see it was three inches long! Surprisingly, the boy never cried out in pain during the procedure.

A young mother brought her terribly dehydrated baby, all skin and bones. Dan called me over to see the severity and said, "It will be difficult to save this baby." If the baby had been in the U.S., she would have been on life support and likely lived. But we were in the bush.

Among our group was news anchor Mike Donahue and his camera-man, Dale Burkholz, sent by KOIN-TV in Portland, Oregon, to cover our work. As Dale videoed the unfolding story, Dr. Dan looked into the camera and said, "This baby might not live through the day."

He treated the child with ORS (Oral Rehydration Solution), one of the greatest discoveries (next to penicillin) used in third-world countries where most children die from dehydration caused by malnutrition and parasites. A ten-cent pack of ORS mixed with a liter of water gives a child the potassium and electrolytes needed to recover from dehydration. Millions of children who were near death have recovered after ORS treatment.

Dr. Dan showed the young mother how to use an eyedropper to continue administering the treatment to her baby. Later I spotted her sitting on the ground, holding her sick child but not giving her the solution. We had learned that the Somalis' religion taught that God's will is to allow the deathly ill to die rather than pursue lifesaving medical help.

I told Dan about the mother, and he reiterated, "It's extremely important to get that solution in the baby, or she'll die!"

I returned to the mother and asked if she would allow me to hold her baby. She agreed, and I sat down, holding the infant, and injected the solution deep into her mouth while rubbing her tiny throat because severe dehydration prevents swallowing. The tragic situation and watching the beautiful baby staring at me with glazed eyes were heartbreaking.

After about ten minutes of force-feeding, Nurse Mary Sue came and checked the baby's pulse and said gravely, "She's fading." Helplessness and heartbreak seized me. In those past short minutes, I had formed a bond with the child.

As Mary Sue held the baby, I wrapped my arms around them and prayed. A crowd began to form around us as though they knew the child was near death. People kept stepping forward to close the baby's eyelids, believing she had died, and I pushed them back, knowing she was still alive. Then the community leader approached me and said, "The baby is dead."

"The baby is not dead!" I cried out, disturbed as more people tried to close the baby's eyelids. "No!" I urged. "God does not want this child to die!" Mary Sue force-fed more antibiotics, but the baby grew worse.

Dan came and checked. "Ron, the baby is near death. Her pulse is very weak."

"No!" I cried again.

Then the baby died.

The weeping mother took her child from Mary Sue's arms, and a group of wailing women escorted them away.

Stunned by the death, I buried my face in my hands and knees and sobbed. Then I walked a distance, needing to be alone, and cried to God, "Why, Lord? Why did this child have to die?" Like the mother and wailing women, I was devastated.

I had seen children die during mission trips around the world, yet I had never before held a dying baby, bonded with her, and watched her die. I understood what our medical volunteers must feel so often as they lose children they're trying to save. The pain of heartbreak could not have been greater had the baby been my own. I couldn't release that darling child from the grip of my soul.

Mary Sue came and put her arm around me, and we both cried. Then Dan joined us and said, "Ron, I see children die, and it's always difficult. I know this child is in the presence of our Lord and completely healed. He wants us to feel the pain to remember how much the children need us."

As we prayed, I asked the Lord, "Reveal to me why the baby died." I knew He would in His time. I will never forget her. Her little face is as vivid in my memory as when I held her. Dan was right. God wanted me to remember my deep grief over the child's death as a reminder of how important it is for people to work together to save as many little ones as possible.

I'm certain I will see that little girl again when I'm called home to heaven.

CHAPTER TWENTY-TWO

MOBILE HELP IN THE UNITED STATES

If anyone does not provide for his relatives, and
especially for his immediate family, he has denied
the faith and is worse than an unbeliever.

— 1 Timothy 5:8

"Oscar's teeth are black," the teacher confided. "I couldn't tell if they're filled or rotted." She'd noticed his difficulty chewing and food falling out of his mouth. Also, mucus constantly ran from his nose. "Other children don't want to sit near him, even at lunchtime. He's the sweetest boy," she added, "and he struggles with schoolwork."

Our dental unit was on the schoolground in the Portland, Oregon, area, and Dr. Lee Emery examined Oscar's mouth. His diagnosis was "many abscesses." The surgical team removed the unsalvageable teeth, and on subsequent visits, they worked to restore and treat Oscar's other teeth. When the treatments were complete, his teacher said, "He's a totally different kid! The dental work was life-changing for him. He's not sick anymore and doing much better in school! I believe it's all because the toxicity is out of his system."

Every month on the first Friday, the mobile dental clinic was at the school. The children looked forward to visiting with the dentists. The teacher had said, "This is a godsend for these children. I'm very grateful."

In 1988, before acquiring the dental unit, I had been amazed to learn how many American citizens like Oscar were falling through the cracks in our nation's healthcare system. Millions couldn't afford to see a dentist and hadn't had teeth care for years, if ever. I wondered if Medical Teams could attract enough volunteer dentists, hygienists, and dental assistants to provide free dental care. By faith, we campaigned for funds to purchase and outfit a mobile dental clinic. We wanted a mobile unit because many had no transportation, and the mobility would enable us to reach more people.

MOEX Corporation, located near our office, made mobile health units. They had a thirty-five-foot trailer available that could be converted into two dental rooms plus an X-ray room.

Medical Teams raised funds to purchase the unit, thanks to corporations, foundations, and individual donors. Then our call went out for volunteer dental professionals. The response was wonderful! One of the first to join us was Dr. Lee Emery. He was on an errand when he saw our building and sign. He'd heard about our mission and wondered if there was a place for him to serve. At that time, our medical director was working on getting the mobile unit ready. Dr. Emery met with him and signed up to work a day each month in the van.

The first dental outreaches included visits to migrant camps where no one earned enough income to afford dental care. The children's teeth were rotting and infected. As a pediatric dentist, Dr. Emery's work with us helped children like Oscar, and his compassion for the children was evident.

Much later, I asked Dr. Emery why he continued volunteering. He answered rather sheepishly, "First, it's selfish. Helping kids who can't afford dental care makes me feel good!" He told me that giving his time had become a way of life for him, and he looked forward to going every time we scheduled him. "Also, I know I'm the last stop for most of those children. I feel that if I don't help, the work won't get done." He loved that his training allowed him to give back to the community.

Early in our dental venture, I'd been concerned about whether I could enlist enough financial support for the unit to be a help. I shouldn't have worried; donors' response was so enormous that we added more mobile units! At this writing, Medical Teams has thirteen state-of-the-art mobile dental units serving the indigent in our country. In addition to migrant camps, our volunteer dental professionals travel to schools, churches, homeless shelters, street kids, and other places where the poor need help. As of 2022, the wonderful clinics on wheels serve nearly nineteen thousand patients a year and are open to anyone who cannot afford dental care.

Never is it too late to get involved with credible ministries like Medical Team that help those in need. Dr. Warren Schafer was nearing the end of a long and productive dental practice when he joined us. His dentistry journey had begun during World War II as a Navy corpsman helping a dentist. After the war, he graduated from dental school with the desire to help others and eventually went into private practice. His volunteer community service began as a firefighter with the Oregon Department of Fish and Wildlife, and he provided free dental care for battered women in the county shelter.

When Dr. Shafer read our mission statement in 1988, a phrase caught his attention: "to demonstrate the love of Christ to those in crisis." As a Christian dentist, he wanted to know if Medical Teams was a genuine mission. He asked questions and saw our work, giving him confidence in what we were doing.

In 1994, he sold his practice and began working in "pure dentistry"— dentistry without all the management concerns. He volunteered nine or more days each month in our mobile unit and spent time requesting the state government give malpractice relief to doctors so more would volunteer.

In an article he wrote, Dr. Schafer shared his feelings about his volunteer work. "I am enjoying every minute. I'm doing dentistry without a care for management. I'm doing what I trained to do. For my salary, I receive thanks, handshakes, hugs, and kisses. I smell the roses all the way."

Dr. Schafer passed from this world, and he's enjoying the retirement account he'd set up in heaven by serving those in need during his earthly life. Only the riches of our good deeds will we carry with us into eternity.

> "Store up for yourselves treasures in heaven."
> — Matthew 6:20

In 1991, Medical Teams was honored by President George H. W. Bush for the work we'd accomplished through our first mobile dental unit. He awarded us the 403rd Daily Point of Light Award. In his letter to us, he wrote,

> We must not allow ourselves to be measured by the sum of our possessions or the size of our bank accounts. The true measure of any individual is found in the way he or she treats others, and the person who regards others with love, respect, and charity holds a priceless treasure in his heart. With that in mind, I have often noted that from now on in America, any definition of a successful life must include serving others. Your efforts provide a shining example of this standard.

CHAPTER TWENTY-THREE

MEDICAL SUPPLIES
FOR THE WORLD

"Ask and it will be given to you."
— Matthew 7:7

D ave Farquhar joined Medical Teams in 1988 when Jean hired him to help with our banquets. Early on, I realized Dave possessed incredible energy, creativity, and fine leadership qualities.

During that time, Medical Teams served the Kurdish refugees and Armenian refugees, and I became aware that many countries lacked basic medical equipment and supplies. Using our good name and reputation, I inquired of factories, hospitals, and other suppliers about donating medical supplies and equipment for us to give to needy countries. And I asked Dave if he would take the challenge to make the vision a reality. He put his heart into developing the program.

Armed with an idea, Dave created a distribution center that is now (2022) sending millions of dollars in medicines, medical equipment, food, and other commodities to many countries, including ours. The distribution center became the largest of its kind on the West Coast.

Dave gathered volunteers who became key to the project's success—such as Fred and Ruth Boruck. They were past retirement age but had no intention of settling down. They desired a meaningful retirement and volunteered their time and skills to help others. Soon they were helping Dave grow the procurement and distribution program. Their volunteer years demonstrated how anyone can use their life skills to help others.

Fred and Ruth had vastly different personalities. Ruth was gentle-hearted and driven to accomplish her goals. When she saw a suffering child, her tears would come. Fred was gentle and quiet, with a twinkle in his eyes that caused people to want to do anything for him. He was my encourager. Whenever the pressures of my work mounted, Fred knew when and what to say—words like, "Ron, don't be discouraged. You're doing a wonderful job. God is very pleased with you."

The precious couple helped us gather millions of donated supplies for those in need. We asked Fred and Ruth to join our staff—they were in their seventies. What an outstanding job they did! For example, Fred procured five million dollars in donated seeds that provided food for millions of poor people in the Russian Republics, Africa, and Southeast Asia. The resulting crops changed the course of countless lives.

While Fred, Ruth, and other volunteers were procuring medicines and food supplies, we attempted to solve a difficult challenge in our warehouse. Most supplies came to us in disorganized lots, and boxes began to stack up. God answered our prayer for help when Jo Bell walked into Medical Teams. She had read about our mission and need for volunteers and answered the call. She organized our sorting area, established ways to keep track of inventory, and got everything shipped to the correct destinations on time and in good repair.

Jo volunteered four to five days a week in our distribution center for over six years! I asked her why she gave so much time, and she answered, "I worked for a living for many years, but now I've found something that's given me purpose."

> Nothing is more fulfilling than finding your purpose and going after it.

Cancer took Jo Bell from us in August 1988—the week after a heart attack took Fred Boruck. Both are with the Lord, enjoying the rewards they'd stored up in heaven. When I visited Jo near her death, she would say, "Oh, Ron, I want so badly to come back and work in the distribution center!" Shortly before she stepped into heaven, she wrote this letter:

> Dear Ron and Jean, bless you for giving me the chance to serve my God and fellow man in such a rewarding way by sorting and packing for Medical Teams. When I re-read my Medical Teams Presidential Citation that hangs on my living room wall, I am so proud to have been one who did serve you well! Please continue the good work, and I'll try to look after you and your "project" from "up there." Have a great day, and do the best job yet in helping others.
>
> My love and blessings,
>
> Jo Bell

Because of Fred, Ruth, Jo, and other volunteers, millions have better lives. Our volunteers who have passed from this life would want two things to continue: Medical Teams shipping life-changing medical supplies and food to the neediest areas around the globe and volunteers of all walks of life and skills stepping forward to help.

People have continued to step up and help. Join them and feel the goodness that comes from serving others. Volunteers have helped bring the family of Medical Teams together. Parents who volunteer demonstrate to their children the importance of helping others, and families who volunteer together are strong.

Medical Teams International Continues to Impact the World

Led by Martha Holley Newsome and her wonderful staff and volunteers, Medical Teams International continues to impact our world. In 2020, Medical Teams served 2.8 million people in twelve countries and sent out 1,207 volunteers. The Distribution Program sent $27 million in care to more than a million people. The total value of care provided was $60 million. In 2022, Medical Teams was serving 1.9 million refugees! As long as volunteers continue to answer God's call to serve, this magnificent work will continue saving and changing lives globally, each volunteer doing their part for the glory of God.

Visit the Medical Teams website: www.medicalteams.org. Read how you can get involved in something greater than yourself. Whether you volunteer your time or help financially, today is the day to make a difference.

CHAPTER TWENTY-FOUR

A NEW CALL IN MY LIFE

Wait for the Lord; be strong and take
heart and wait for the Lord.

— Psalm 27:14

Since founding Medical Teams in 1979, I'd gone to work with excitement every day for what God would do. Eighteen years quickly passed as I watched the many wonderful things God did.

But in that eighteenth year, 1997, something strange began. I struggled in the mornings, lacking zeal about going into the office. I had no idea why. *I love Medical Teams, so what's wrong with me?*

Sometime during that struggle, I had an almost overwhelming feeling that it was time for me to leave Medical Teams. Trusting that God had something else in mind for me, I presented my resignation to the board, though with a trembling voice. I don't know if they were shocked by my resignation, but I was. They asked me to stay in the capacity of president emeritus. I agreed to two years. I wasn't sure what God would have me do after, but if I had learned anything through the years, it was that God would give me direction in His time and way.

In 1999, I was sitting in my office when a memory popped in. During my years with Medical Teams, other ministries would call and ask how we were able to raise funds to finance our enormous projects. Each caller struggled with the funding part of ministry work. I would offer advice but had little time to spend with them.

Following the memory was a sudden strong urge to help small ministries understand how to grow their missions. I had been in their shoes early in ministry, unaware how to raise funds for Medical Teams, and a good Samaritan came along my road in the 1980s and stopped to help me multiple times.

When I had been asked to investigate some needs in Baja, California, I didn't want to drive that distance. I thought of the mission of pilots based in Redlands, California, Mission Aviation Fellowship, that had flown our teams into the remote areas of Ethiopia and Kenya. I called and asked if they had someone who would fly me to Baja for a research trip. They referred me to Jack Walker, who agreed. Little did I know that he was my good Samaritan and would change my approach to fundraising.

Mission Aviation pilots are the bravest you could ever meet. Jack had spent years flying into the bush in Mexico and South America, delivering food and supplies and sharing the gospel of Jesus Christ. Every time a pilot went out, they risked their lives. Remote landing strips were small and crude. Pilots had died flying into such places, and native Indians had killed others.

During Medical Teams' time in Oaxaca, three Mission Aviation Fellowship planes crashed, two of them killing the pilots and five Indians. In the other, the pilot survived. They are indeed among the bravest people I've ever known. Throughout Jack's flying career, he had crashed once and had several close calls.

At some point, Mission Aviation Fellowship asked Jack if he would take over their fundraising. He did and continued for years after.

When I learned that Jack knew a great deal about fundraising, I asked him if he would give me help. His response was, "Anytime, Ron."

In the early years, I made many calls to Jack for fundraising knowledge. He never turned me down and never said he was too busy. On occasion, he even flew to Portland to give me one-on-one training and never asked anything in return. He wouldn't allow Medical Teams to pay him. His help was his gift to us, straight from God.

Sitting in my office with those memories, I felt that God's next mission for me was to help small ministries in Oregon for no fee, giving my time and knowledge about fundraising. As with all new endeavors, I had many questions. God was about to answer them.

The ministry's unfolding started over breakfast with a longtime friend and donor to Medical Teams. Dale Stockamp was a successful businessman. I told him I wanted to help Christian ministries in Oregon grow by teaching them to use biblical fundraising principles. I shared how Jack Walker had helped me and never charged and that I felt led to do the same for struggling ministries.

Dale responded that he too wanted to help Christian ministries. We both viewed investing in people's training as a great leverage opportunity. I would offer training in biblical fundraising, and Dale would offer his business experience. He would create a business model that would allow us to track how the small organizations were doing as they implemented the training.

Two questions remained: Do ministries need our help, and would they respond to our training? Our next step was to contact a ministry.

While searching for ministries in the Portland area, I discovered Union Gospel Mission and placed a call to them. Kevin Campbell answered. I'd not met Kevin, and I introduced myself. "Hi Kevin, this is Ron Post."

"Oh, hi, Ron." He seemed to recognize my name. I asked him if their mission could use training to facilitate their fundraising efforts.

After a pause, Kevin said, "Ron, you may not believe this, but our whole staff spent the morning on their knees together, asking God to answer whether we should continue this seventy-year-old mission or close the doors." He then shared that the ministry was under a million dollar debt accrued by a former director and had no way to pay.

My jaw dropped.

I was further stunned when he added, "As I was praying with our group, I specifically asked God to send us someone like Ron Post."

"Kevin! Are you kidding me?"

"No, Ron, that's exactly what I prayed." We were both in awe of God's uniting Spirit and His faithfulness as our provider. "Do you think you can help us?" he asked.

Fighting back my tears, I said, "Yes, Kevin, I think I can."

God is so good.

Back in 1979, when God pulled me from my easy chair to take a medical team to help the Cambodian refugees, His mission was clear to me. Twenty years later, He'd done it again—this time pulling me at age sixty from my office chair at Medical Teams.

As a result of my conversation with Kevin, Mission Increase, conceived by God, was born. Dale and his wife, Gail, were on board with me. When Dale and I first talked about our ministry desires, he shared that Gail was an incredible prayer warrior who would want to be part of the endeavor. We each desired to help other Christian ministries grow and increase.

God was about to use Mission Increase to accomplish something never before done in U.S. history: a nonprofit organization would offer free biblical fundraising training to another nonprofit. Characteristically, nonprofits compete for donor dollars. Mission Increase would blaze a new trail. We loved the challenge, knowing the Lord alone had opened this door.

He had brought three willing people together who would each manage a different aspect of the assignment. Dale had the skills to run a large organization and see the big picture. Gail would keep the mission on track through prayer, a vital foundational requirement for any success-ful mission. At that time, we didn't know that Gail would eventually serve as our national prayer person. God had given me the gift of organization and the skills to train ministries. With God at the helm, we began a mission of critical importance in our country: financially stabilizing and growing ministries called by God to serve "the least of these" (Matthew 25:40).

Jean's prior work organizing yearly banquets added an indispensable tool as part of Mission Increase's training material. She had created a how-to manual for successfully organizing fundraising banquets!

I taught the staff of Union Gospel Mission to view donors not simply as givers but as *champions* partnering with their mission. I taught the principles of creating unique events; using direct mail, direct phone calls, and direct visits; reconnecting with lapsed champions; and asking them to match other gifts.

After a year and a half, Kevin called and shared an astonishing update. "Ron, you won't believe this! We're debt free!"

God is so good! They had retired the million dollar debt, and we rejoiced with them.

While talking with the Union Gospel Mission's CEO, Bill Russell, I asked him what he planned to do with the dilapidated building connected to their building. He said, "I hope to one day tear it down and build a larger facility. We want to house more people in our LifeChange program."

"Why don't you do that now?" I asked.

"The project will cost millions to tear down and build a three-story building."

"Do it," I urged him and showed him how to create a capital campaign.

Bill compiled the cost figures and concluded the project would require eight million dollars!

Nothing is too great for God and for those who put their trust in Him! Bill is an outstanding leader and believer in the power of Christ. He, his board, and his staff believed together that God would accomplish the massive goal.

> Jesus said, "I tell you that if two of you on earth agree about anything they ask for, it will be done for them by my Father in heaven." — Matthew 18:19

The Lord answered their prayers and met the eight million dollar need. Remember that the rehab campaign began briefly after nearly closing the mission. As I write this book, Union Gospel Mission serves from a beautiful three-story building worth ten million dollars.

Growing Mission Increase

> Now it is required that those who have been given
> a trust must prove faithful. — 1 Corinthians 4:2

Dale, Gail, and I saw the success of Union Gospel Mission as God's affirmation that we were to help more faith-based ministries learn how to grow and increase. Our motto is, "We help ministries grow by offering teaching, coaching, and consulting rooted in a biblical approach to fundraising—all at no cost to the ministries."

Early on, we brought Dave Farquhar in to help formulate training models. He had worked with me at Medical Teams International to build our World Distribution Center and fundraising program.

To help ministries increase their fundraising, Dave designed a variety of workshops that emphasized viewing donors as their missions' champions, how to engage with them, how to engage them in the ministry, and the joy of giving with the right heart. We also wanted mission leaders and staff to understand that simply asking for money was no way to create a lasting relationship with those who give. So, Dave developed a class called Transformational Giving, built on Jesus's words:

> "It is more blessed to give than to receive."
> — Acts 20:35

When a ministry's staff implements what they learned through Mission Increase, they experience tremendous ministry growth and a *community* relationship between them and their champions.

As we trained ministries, we learned they felt isolated because of little or no contact with other Christian nonprofits. With Mission Increase alongside them and our workshops bringing ministries together—which was a first—they no longer felt alone. Our training also emphasized seeing other ministries as *partners* rather than competitors for donor dollars, which was also a first. Friendships formed across ministries as they encouraged one another. What a change of dynamics!

Also extraordinary, Mission Increase brought nonprofit ministries together with local churches. Churches have since seen the benefits of working in partnership with other ministries, understanding that both *are* the global church—the body of Christ, as explained in 1 Corinthians 12. Christian ministries and churches are experiencing how much more they can accomplish by viewing their various work for Christ as one body with many parts. Working together, ministries and churches are more effective in their causes.

As I trained Christian nonprofits, I felt like part of their ministries, as though God had saved the best for last—though *all* my mission experiences have been beyond words.

By teaching ministries across the nation how to grow, Mission Increase achieves our greater goal: providing more food, clothing, shelter, medical care, and other needed services that reflect Jesus's love and care, creating the path to reach more hearts for Jesus Christ, offering the food of the gospel and the clothing of God's righteousness:

> To bestow on them a crown of beauty instead of ashes, the oil of joy instead of mourning, and a garment of praise instead of a spirit of despair. They will be called oaks of righteousness, a planting of the Lord for the display of his splendor. — Isaiah 61:3

Onward

Mission Increase experienced enormous growth when God brought Dan Davis to us. Dan had served years with Medical Teams

International as our accountant, beginning right after college. Early on, Jean and I saw something incredibly special in the young man, and we quickly grew to love him as a son. At this point, Dan was no longer working with Medical Teams, so I asked him to work for Mission Increase.

Dan has many gifts, including finding well-qualified people to help further Mission Increase's vision. Dan now serves as president. Under his leadership, his team is growing training centers in communities nationwide.

To begin a Mission Increase Training Center in a city, we attract the city's local potential partners who will see the tremendous value of our training for their city. Local partners working in sync with local ministries allow the partners to leverage their giving and see God's kingdom work grow.

Though I now sit on the sidelines, I'm Mission Increase's number-one cheerleader. I love the staff of wonderful brothers and sisters. I'm amazed by their accomplishments! God has entrusted every staff member to be faithful in the calling He placed on their lives. Including field staff across the country and those at our National Resource Center in Oregon, Mission Increase has nearly fifty staff members (2022) training thousands of nonprofit ministries. With Dale, Gail, Dan, and a wonderful board of directors, this Christ-led mission is impacting millions of lives here and around the world.

Mission Increase has multiplied many times over. In 2021, the staff trained over 3,300 ministries, and the ministries' income grew by $475 million collectively! The God-sized goal of Mission Increase toward serving the needs of more people is a combined increase of over $1 billion annually. Consider the significant impact this will make for those in need in our country and worldwide!

I invite you to visit the Mission Increase website to see the exciting work: www.missionincrease.org.

CHAPTER TWENTY-FIVE

EARTHLY AND HEAVENLY

LEGACIES

A good person leaves an inheritance
for their children's children.

— Proverbs 13:22

Leaving tangible legacies is good, as shown in the Bible. The result of arduous work is inheritance, blessing your children after you've left this world. Hopefully, they'll pass an earthly legacy to their children. But what about leaving a heavenly legacy for our children to follow? We must revisit and remind ourselves and others of the wisdom of Matthew 6:19–21:

> "Do not store up for yourselves treasures on earth . . . But store up for yourselves treasures in heaven . . . For where your treasure is, there your heart will be also."

May this passage be our guiding light, reminding us we cannot take anything from this earth, but we can enter the treasures we've stored in heaven—the best legacy of wisdom we can pass on to our children and theirs.

I've thought about all the activities that have brought me happiness over the years: business ventures, singing and performing rock-and-roll and gospel, fishing, and vegetable gardening. And I've thought about the surprising honors that blessed me, like the honorary degrees from Lewis & Clark College in Portland, Oregon, and Northwest Christian University in Eugene, Oregon. All these and more are abundantly meaningful aspects of my earthly life, yet a question nagged at me: *What kind of lasting legacy will I leave behind?*

Years after beginning Medical Teams, I told a dear friend, John Castles, a story about Medical Teams' work in Ethiopia. He stopped me and said, "Ron, what a wonderful legacy you're leaving for your family and all of us who know you."

I paused, taken aback. "I hadn't thought about that before!" I exclaimed. Then John said something else I've not forgotten.

"Having the opportunity of wealth yet devoting your life to helping others is the best legacy one could leave behind." His words impacted my heart in a way few others had. His affirmation still means so much because I deeply admire John. He's a longtime trustee of The Murdock Trust, which gives millions of dollars in grants to organizations in Northwest America. John and his wife, Sarah, volunteer for several ministries, inspiring people to greater faith and good deeds. They're beautiful examples of selflessness, helping others succeed. The legacy they've built will bless their family long after they pass from this life.

"John, I appreciate what you said," I replied. "I'm content with the work of helping those in need. I've not felt more peace doing anything else, and I wouldn't exchange seeing precious children restored from near death for all the riches I could have amassed."

After finishing this book's manuscript, I went through a long period of searching my heart about whether to publish. Eventually, I decided to pass the unpublished manuscript to my family as a tangible legacy.

I sent a copy to John as a dear friend who treasured the work and experiences of Medical Teams. When he later called, I expected a polite response because that's who John is. So, I was again taken aback when he exclaimed, "Ron, this is an inspiring book and must be published!" He shared other reasons for publishing, but his first statement was enough. Without his encouragement, you would not be reading this book. John is one of the greatest encouragers I've had in life—that's who John is and what motivates people who listen to him.

God loves when we encourage others. That encouragement builds their confidence and costs us nothing.

> Encourage one another daily, as long as it is called "Today." — Hebrews 3:13

Encourage your family and friends to believe they can do more than they think.

Early in my adult years, I wanted to become as wealthy as my relatives. While financial legacies, security, and retirement are worthy goals, they were once my *only* goals, and my heart felt lacking.

Learning this vital truth shifted my mindset and decisions:

> Wealth does not bring or create lasting fulfillment, peace, and contentment.

God's Word showed me that our priority should not be earthly wealth but the good we do with what we have. Since heaven is my destination, I wanted to care for all that God cares for.

> A good name is more desirable than great riches; to be esteemed is better than silver or gold. — Proverbs 22:1

Pursuing a life of meaning and purpose brings ultimate satisfaction, a legacy of compassionate service, and esteem that motivates others to serve. Think of Mother Teresa's esteem, all the giving people mentioned in this book, those you admire in your life for their dedicated service to the needy, and those esteemed in God's Word for giving themselves sacrificially—the greatest being Jesus Christ.

I know wealthy people who are esteemed, not because of their wealth but because they share their wealth to help the poor. They understand their life purpose: to love and serve others as Jesus did.

Our Inner Programming

> We are God's handiwork, created in Christ Jesus to do good works, which God prepared in advance for us to do.
> — Ephesians 2:10

I've given much thought to that verse, which says "we." Every person is God's workmanship, created and prepared to do good works. Does "prepared" mean programmed? Well, God programmed our DNA to do good works.

Think of the verse as a computer programmer might: God wrote a love program and installed it in our DNA, along with our free will to either use His programming or ignore it. He doesn't force us but continually calls us to use the gifts He programmed in us for His purpose: loving Him and bringing Him joy and glory by loving and caring for others as Jesus did.

> It is God who works in you to will and to act in order to fulfill his good purpose.
> — Philippians 2:13

You may ask, "Is that why I feel so good when I serve others?" Yes, He also programmed us to feel good when we "act in order to fulfill his good purpose." I've witnessed and experienced the joy of making a positive difference that our volunteers feel after a mission trip. Though they went to help others have better lives, they returned feeling incredibly blessed, which is how all our volunteers and donors feel. Such fulfillment has little to do with beliefs and everything to do with how God programmed us as human beings. Throughout history, we've witnessed that both Christians and non-Christians feel blessed when helping others, which is why Jesus said,

> "It is more blessed to give than to receive."
> — Acts 20:35

An example is a young mother carrying her child while carrying a bag of groceries that suddenly breaks. Her purchases fall out, and those nearby *instinctively* feel prompted to help her (God's programming at work). Then free will kicks in, presenting the choice to help the mother or pass her by. Those who help experience joy, and those who pass her experience opposite feelings, like conviction, guilt, and regret.

A 2022 *Healthline* article shared a scientific brain chemistry study proving that "Helping others . . . helps release a mood-enhancing hormone known as oxytocin." They interviewed the study author, Dr. Paul J. Zak, director of the Center for Neuroeconomics Studies at Claremont Graduate University in California, who said, "It's really one of the most 'wow' and bullet-proof [results] I've seen in 20 years of being in the lab." And he added, "People who are happiest live the longest too." [9]

When doing what God designed us to do, we're naturally happier, healthier, and more content.

---

99 Moira McCarthy, "Helping Others Can Make You Happier as You Age: Here's Why," *Health News*, *April 20, 2022. Healthline: https://www.healthline.com/health-news/helping-others-can-make-you-happier-as-you-age-heres-why.*

Global and local ministries need volunteers. There are needs in your community, at your church, and among your neighbors—people who are hurting badly and need practical help and the love of Jesus demonstrated. It's never too late to help, but have you begun that fulfilling journey?

Life slips by so fast. We can easily get caught up in life and forget what's most important. A quote reads, "Life is like a coin. You can spend it any way you wish, but you can only spend it once." [10] I wanted to be sure I was spending my coin wisely. If you aren't, you can choose right now to change. You don't know how long you have left in this life or how long those in desperate need will survive, so begin serving now, no matter your age.

Many senior citizens serve with Medical Teams. Ansgar Schei, a dear friend who has passed away, was a car dealer who served his church as an elder and organized an annual fundraising banquet for Medical Teams for years. He'd lived in his small town for over eighty years and accumulated many friends. He persuaded them to sponsor the banquet tables and fill them with people. Of the few thousand town residents, approximately 250 attended the annual banquet, which (accumulatively) raised well over $200,000! Ansgar loved organizing the banquets, which brought him happiness and fulfillment because he knew the results were changing lives worldwide for the better.

I love football and enjoy watching a Sunday afternoon game. As a young boy, we had only a radio for entertainment, and I loved listening to the great athlete and sportscaster Tom Harmon. He'd tell wonderful stories of athletes' great feats. I loved hearing about the football player Red Grange of Illinois, nicknamed "The Galloping Ghost." With a name like that, a young boy's heart couldn't help but beat faster hearing it.

---

10 Attributed to Lillian Dickson, *These My People: Serving Christ Among the Mountain People of Formosa.*

Tom told how Red made history on October 18, 1924, playing against Michigan. The first time Red got the ball, he ran 95 yards for a touchdown; the second time, 67 yards; the third time, 56 yards; and the fourth touchdown, 44 yards. He had the ball four times, scored four times, and covered 262 yards, all without being tackled! An amazing feat. In 2008, ESPN named Red the best college football player of all time, and in 2011 the Big Ten Network named him the Greatest Big Ten Icon.

Though Red Grange got the applause and his esteemed name went into the record book, he hadn't performed the astonishing feat alone. He had a great team of players who did their unique parts that knocked opposing players out of the way so he could make those touchdowns.

Volunteers operate in the same way.

You're never alone when volunteering. Your teammates assist you all the way. Whether serving with Medical Teams or a civic club, school, battered women's shelter, homeless shelter, food bank, children's hospital, shut-in meal delivery, senior center, or church, teammates are there to support you and one another.

Industrialist and philanthropist Andrew Carnegie defined teamwork as "the fuel that allows common people to attain uncommon results."[11]

Teams of ordinary people attaining unbelievable results in the U.S. and globally have been the experiences of my life's work—the lame walking, the blind seeing, the sick healing, the poor eating, the widow and orphan receiving care, and the hopeless gaining renewed spirits.

The truth is, I've never seen people stand higher or feel greater than when they're on the train bound for mercy—a place where the receiver and giver become one.

---

11 Andrew Carnegie, quoted in David W. DeFord, *1000 Brilliant Achievement Quotes: Advice from the World's Wisest* (Omaha, NE: Ordinary People Can Win! 2004), 185.

> Dear children, let us not love with words or
> tongue but with actions and in truth.
> —1 John 3:18

A life not lived as God designed is not true living! Actions do speak louder than words.

> First, I was dying to finish high school and start college; and then I was dying to finish college and start working; and then I was dying for my children to grow old enough for school, so I could return to work, and then I was dying to retire . . . and now, I am dying . . . and suddenly I realize I forgot to live! — Unknown

Have you wondered how God can use you? Perhaps you've had moments when you felt Him impress you to do something specific, but you didn't know how or where to begin, so you did nothing. As you've witnessed through my life journey, I often felt inadequate for the tasks ahead and wondered how God could use me. I encourage you to begin as I did: take one step of faith. Volunteer at a nonprofit dedicated to helping those in need.

> We make a living by what we do, but we make a life
> by what we do for others

I had waited years to discover that life is more than working to accumulate material things and doing entertaining activities. Once I finally stepped out of my comfort zone, God allowed me to see the opportunities. Miracles were in my future. Miracles are in your future too if you take a step of faith to serve others. Had I stayed seated, I would not have witnessed Fredrico's regained sight, Ramon's corrected cleft lip and palate, Oscar's repaired teeth, and millions of children and families receiving lifesaving help. I would not have witnessed our compassionate, dedicated teams and volunteers turning hopelessness into hope.

CHAPTER TWENTY-SIX

WEALTH AND STATUS

It is God who works in you to will and to
act in order to fulfill his good purpose.

— Philippians 2:13

For many years, my heart desired stardom as a singer with the second Del Vikings group, then the split-off group La Chords, and as a solo artist. In favor of singing with the La Chords, I turned down Gus Backus's invitation to partner with him to record songs in German—and he went on to become a well-known, highly-regarded singer and actor in Germany. When I came to know Jesus and gave my life to Him, I was thrilled to sing for God's glory.

Now, the rest of that story.

In 1978, at the church Jean and I attended in Salem, Oregon, I was in rehearsal season with our Singing Christmas Tree that performed every year. I was excited that the church had invited Doug Oldham to fly from Tennessee to perform with us. You may recall his name; he became famous in the seventies for recording Bill Gaither's songs. He was the number-one gospel singer in the U.S. for ten years. Doug has since passed, but my memory of that gentleman is vivid.

Two days before the performance, Doug called our director to let him know he could not sing his part of the performance but would be glad to narrate the program. I got a call about the situation, and the caller asked me to take his place. I was surprised and excited.

I asked the caller what the role would involve. He answered, "You'll need to learn three songs and an acting part within two days."

"Are you kidding me?" I was stunned by the lack of time. "How could anyone be expected to learn all that in less than two days?"

"I know, Ron, but it's vital," he urged. "We cannot take those parts out of the program."

I took a huge gulp (of faith) and told him I'd try. Never before had I faced memorizing so much in such a brief time. By the grace of God, I did it!

Doug arrived the day before the program, ready to practice the narration. I had the pleasure of meeting him and sitting with him several times.

On opening night, between the two performances, he said, "Ron, you have a good voice. If you'd like to come to Nashville, I'll put you in a group and get you a recording contract."

What an opportunity! I was overjoyed and said I'd speak to Jean and get back to him.

When telling Jean, I was almost jumping up and down. I loved singing gospel because God spoke to me through music, and here was an opportunity to sing to the world! I asked Jean what she thought about a trip to Nashville, and she agreed. I called Doug and accepted his offer.

He arranged for us to stay at the Opryland Hotel, and Jean and I spent a week in Nashville. We especially enjoyed touring the city. My mother's family was from Tennessee, which added even more value to our time there.

As Doug and I talked, he learned about my business background and surprised me again. He asked if I would move there to be his business manager. A dual opportunity! I could sing and take care of Doug's business affairs. The idea was thrilling.

The night before we returned to Oregon, Jean and I sat in our hotel room, discussing the future. I could tell she felt uncomfortable. I asked, "How do you feel about moving here?"

She hesitated and said honestly, "I'm sorry, honey, but I don't feel good about moving here. How do you feel?" I could hardly get my words out.

"I don't know why, but I don't feel led to move here either." I also felt as if someone had hit my heart with a sledgehammer. My dream was to sing, and Doug's invitation offered to fulfill that. Yet something in me felt unsettled. We flew out the next day with my heart weighing heavy.

After giving myself a few days to deliberate, I called Doug and declined, which was extremely hard. He was very gracious, agreeing that the move wouldn't be right if it weren't God's will for us. He said he'd welcome us if our thoughts ever changed. I hung up, feeling deflated, my spirit's oxygen sucked out. *Why, God? This is what I've always wanted. Why can't I do this?*

God would answer the next year when He'd call me from my easy chair to take that first step of faith to organize and lead a team of medical volunteers to help the Cambodian refugees. I would never have imagined such a drastic turn in my life nor the extraordinary experiences and fulfillment ahead!

In hindsight, I understand. Earthly stardom paled in the glorious light of Jesus that shone from the faces of millions since helped by Medical Teams. Had I ignored God's call in me and partnered with Gus Backus or Doug Oldham, I would have failed in either because God had a different plan for my life and Jean's—an utterly jaw-dropping plan that would extend and expand for the rest of our life together.

> Remember the Lord your God. He is the one who gives you power to be successful, in order to fulfill the covenant he confirmed to your ancestors with an oath. — Deuteronomy 8:18

You may be asking what I mean by "I would have failed." Our heavenly Father's plans are always better than ours, even when we don't understand His ways. He directs our steps, and when we choose to follow Him, He ensures our success, just as he did for my friend Doug Oldham.

God sent Moses into the wilderness to live a poor and humble life in preparation for him to change the course of the Jewish people. God would direct him to go before the king of Egypt (a huge deal) and demand the king let God's enslaved people go. But Moses had a speech impediment! He was certain he didn't have what it would take to accomplish what God had called him to. He asked God, "Who am I that I should go to Pharaoh?" (Exodus 3:11).

I don't know about you, but I've often felt as Moses must have. *Who am I to do everything necessary to organize a pioneering journey and take a medical team to help thousands of Cambodian refugees? Who am I to lead such an organization that rapidly grew into Medical Teams International? I don't even have a college diploma!* But one day, God woke this old hardhead to something vital I needed to remember from His Word. Jesus often approached the seemingly unable and unlikely to carry out His plans in extraordinary ways. Jesus's disciples consisted of fishermen, tradesmen, businessmen, a political anarchist, a thief, and even a well-known and feared murderer of Christians whom He called and transformed to follow Him.

He called me—uneducated but willing—and gave me every tool I needed, exactly when and where I needed it, to accomplish His purpose, just as He had for Moses and countless other common, ordinary people throughout history. We have experienced His divine empowerment to accomplish what seemed impossible. As Mother Teresa said, "Glory to God!"

Though He created us each with unique gifts and purposes, He designed us to work seamlessly together as the body of Christ.

> Just as a body, though one, has many parts, . . . so it is with Christ. . . . God has placed the parts . . . just as he wanted them to be. . . . You are the body of Christ, and each one of you is a part of it. — 1 Corinthians 12:12, 18, 27

Christ-followers have in common their love for Him, compassion and love for others, and the yes to get up, go, and love "the least of these." Christ's plan for my life would not make me a star or wealthy man in the eyes of others, but His plan gave me far greater riches than this world could ever offer. I love this verse:

> The world and its desires pass away, but whoever does the will of God lives forever. — 1 John 2:17

Stardom, status, money, and other earthly things will eventually disappear, but God's eternal rewards for those who follow Him last forever. I have not regretted following Christ. Borrowing the words of the apostle Paul . . .

> My life is worth nothing to me unless I use it for finishing the work assigned me by the Lord Jesus. — Acts 20:24 NLT

Years ago, I wrote my purpose inside my Bible. I share this for you to consider for your life.

> The Purpose for My Life:
> To seek Him
> To know Him
> To serve Him
> To share Him

Whether wealthy, middle-class, poor, educated, or uneducated, the following questions apply to each of us:

- What am I doing with my life?
- What am I building for future generations and eternity?

Have you discovered God's purpose for you, and are you living out your assignments to complete His purpose?

> A person may think their own ways are right, but the Lord weighs the heart. To do what is right and just is more acceptable to the Lord than sacrifice. — Proverbs 21:2–3

Gratitude

While serving through Medical Teams, I routinely asked our accounting department to be sure every donor received an acknowledgment for their gifts. I also asked the staff to give the prepared notes of thanks to me so I could add my expressions of gratitude to each.

Having seen and experienced the sacrificial giving of others, I felt grateful for every gift the ministry received. Each gift and giver were a blessing. Sometimes we received a twenty-five dollar donation with a note written by a shaky hand: "I wish I could give more, but I receive only a small Social Security check, and this is all I can give." My heart would well up, and I'd weep. My handwritten response to the dear person let them know how special they were and how blessed we were to have them as champions of the wonderful ministry.

Years ago I was sitting at my desk when my assistant came in and told me my good friend Harley was there to see me. I had in the past taken this fine man on a tour of our work in Mexico. I got up and welcomed him and his family into my office.

After a bit of small talk, he said, "Ron, we want to help with the splendid work you're doing in Mexico." He handed me a check. I glanced at it and thought, *Wow! How wonderful! A gift of $25,000!* Then I looked again and saw more zeros: $250,000! I was speechless. Our Program Director and Jean were in the room, and everyone wept with gratitude.

At that time, Harley was about eighty-five years old, living in a home built back in the forties. When I'd first visited him there, I discovered he heated the rooms with wood, and to turn on the hall light required reaching up to the socket and tightening the bulb. His folks had been pioneers who'd owned wooded acres that Harley had worked as an adult to earn his living. He was a joy! Harley is now with the Lord in heaven, and I miss his wonderful smile and cheerful outlook. He was one of the dearest men I'd ever met. I cherish his memory.

On the one hand, Medical Teams received gifts of $25, and on the other hand, $250,000. Which one blessed me more? Both. I was incredibly blessed knowing the givers' tender hearts for the poor, and I knew God was pleased with every gift and giver.

> Each of you should give what you have decided in your heart to give, not reluctantly or under compulsion, for God loves a cheerful giver. And God is able to bless you abundantly, so that in all things at all times, having all that you need, you will abound in every good work. — 2 Corinthians 9:6–8

He doesn't care how much we have but what we do with what He's given us. He knows our hearts and the gifts we can give those in need—our time, skills, and money wrapped in love and compassion. We're each called to give with joy and gratitude for what He has given us—not occasionally but as a way of life.

Serving

I asked a pastor friend David Shimeall where he had pastored. His response surprised me. "I haven't always been a pastor." He shared that he had gone to seminary and begun pastoring *after* his teaching career!

"You mean you taught until you retired and then went to seminary and pastored?"

"Yes," he answered. "I felt called to become a pastor after retiring"

But his story got even better. After retiring as a lead pastor, he served as a visitation pastor. What an example for us all to consider! I believe my friend David understood priorities very well, like the apostle Paul:

> I consider my life worth nothing to me, if only I may finish the race and complete the task the Lord Jesus has given me— testifying to the gospel of God's grace. — Acts 20:24

Pastor David could have retired to live his life in whatever way he wanted, and he chose to encourage and pray for the sick and visit shut-ins. He continues to serve others and would encourage us all to remember these words of Christ:

> Whatever you did for one of the least of these brothers and sisters of mine, you did for me. — Matthew 25:40

Remember, we make a living by what we do, but we make a life by what we do for others.

Are you making a life by what you do for others? You may say, "Ron, I made my living, and now I'm going to do what I want." You can do what you want, but whatever that is, does it give your life meaning and purpose? Life is brief. You'll believe this later if you don't already.

> Whatever you do, work at it with all your heart as working for the Lord, . . .since you know that you will receive an inheritance from the Lord as a reward. It is the Lord Christ you are serving. — Colossians 3:23–24

My friend Joe Silleman served in Vietnam and later as a firefighter in Orange County, California. Knowing Joe, I believe he became a firefighter because he wanted to serve others. He's now retired, but I've seen him quietly serving others. He volunteers for whatever is needed at his church and serves his community with the Veterans of Foreign Wars. Joe takes part as a Color Guard in parades, and in preparation for Veterans Day, he works a full day putting hundreds of American flags in the local cemetery. He also spends hours calling fellow veterans to check on them and comfort them when they're troubled.

> A person is considered righteous by what they do and not by faith alone. . . . As the body without the spirit is dead, so faith without deeds is dead." — James 2:24, 26

Through many years, I've spoken with hundreds of volunteers and heard a common theme: "I love my work, but I get the greatest joy when I'm volunteering." Many volunteer during their career years and continue volunteering in their retirement years. Why? Because God instilled in each of us the desire to help others, and the earthly rewards are like no other: true fulfillment and joy.

> The righteous will flourish like a palm tree, they will grow like a cedar of Lebanon; planted in the house of the Lord, they will flourish in the courts of our God. *They will still bear fruit in old age*, they will stay fresh and green, proclaiming, The Lord is upright; he is my Rock, and there is no wickedness in him.
> — Psalm 92:12–15 (author emphasis)

As I was reading God's Word, a verse jumped out at me:

Did you get that phrase "old age"? We can still bear fruit in *old age*! We're never too old to serve in some way.

I ended my official involvement in ministry in 2019, but did I still have a purpose and more to give? Yes! There are many ways I can continue serving God by serving others. I can encourage and lift people's spirits, share my relationship with Christ, and share ministry stories of God's provisions, faithfulness, and miracles. I can advise, mentor younger people, and even mow the church lawn. (Well, my age may not permit that!)

> Our older years should be a joy because we have more time to serve others.

After my dear Jean retired from ministry, she was sitting in church one Sunday, reading the bulletin, and noticed the listed names and addresses of the ill and those shut in. For years after, she made it her mission to write a card every week to each, letting them know they were loved and in her prayers. People are greatly blessed to know they're loved, valued, and in someone's thoughts and prayers.

My beloved Jean is now living in a memory care facility. She has lived a long and meaningful life of purpose. God is well pleased with her. She's been my partner in life and ministry for an exceptionally long time. We have walked through fires yet haven't been burned, as the apostle Paul expressed to believers in Jesus:

> We are hard pressed on every side, but not crushed; perplexed, but not in despair; persecuted, but not abandoned; struck down, but not destroyed. We always carry around in our body the death of Jesus, so that the life of Jesus may also be revealed in our body.
> — 2 Corinthians 4:8–10

The commitment Jean and I made to the Lord long ago is still strong. Though Jean's days grow dimmer, she still cares for others. One day at mealtime, she sat with a resident who was in great pain. Jean put her hand on his and asked, "Steve, may I pray for you?" He was so grateful for her moment of care.

> Dear senior citizens, though our eyes grow dim and our bodies weak, God can still use what we have remaining.

King David knew age was creeping up on him, and his concern was that God might not be as happy with him if he could no longer be strong in battle. He said to the Lord, "Do not cast me away when I am old; do not forsake me when my strength is gone. . . . Even when I am old and gray, do not forsake me, O God, till I declare your power to the next generation, your might to all who are to come" (Psalm 71:9, 18).

221

Clearly, David was not intending to retire from serving God or to forget all God had done for him. As he aged, he shouted his joy for the Lord even more!

Both young and old have something in common: We're all aging! The difference is that the aged know how fast time passes, while the youth haven't yet noticed. Most of us have an awakening moment when we realize we're no longer young. But do we have an awakening that we can still serve others?

As seniors, we may believe the younger generations don't want to hear what we have to share and feel that they're not hearing us. But occasionally, one of my grandchildren will send me a note or tell me they love and appreciate the things I share with them. They do hear what we say!

We must model serving others to the younger generations because many are not being taught to serve. We can serve young people and adults by sharing and showing servanthood to those in need. Those younger than we are in need of the wisdom we've gained. As long as we have breath, we can serve the needy nearby and abroad in some capacity. I invite you to join me in prayer:

Lord, let me be a light and encouragement for others. Let me be Your eyes so people can see You through me, and let me be Your hands to those who need Your touch. Help me know and complete my assignment 'til my last breath.

MY HOPE FOR YOU

For the Lord gives wisdom, and from his mouth
come knowledge and understanding.

— Proverbs 2:6

The day I began to write this book, doubts clouded my mind. I asked God if sharing my life stories was truly His next step for me. That morning, the Bible verse I "happened" to read first was Psalm 102:18: "Let this be written for a future generation, that a people not yet created may praise the Lord" (NIV). As a believer in God's divine leading, I knew the answer had come from Him.

I hope my story has given you new perspectives you'll apply to your life, including how precious and necessary you are to the greater purpose: helping others practically and spiritually.

I hope my journey has motivated or further inspired you to be a winner for Christ, valiantly finishing the race He set before you.

You are not alone if you haven't yet discovered your unique, God-planted gifts and purpose. Be assured that you will uncover these as you study God's Word, have ongoing conversations with Him in prayer, and serve alongside others.

If you're not yet serving, I hope my experiences have assured you that you *can* do *anything* you set your heart and mind to in Christ Jesus and overcome whatever is holding you back. Exchange obstacles, including fears and anxieties, with faith in God's power, strength, and direction—and take the first step. Make calls to nonprofits whose mission is helping the needy and ask, "How can I help?" Then go and serve.

Will today be your day to become unchained from your past and find freedom with Christ for your future? Will today be the day you rise from your easy chair and become all God created and desires you to be? You can trust Him. He is faithful, loves you like no other, and has called you.

Dear Reader,

I pray this book has been a blessing and a help to you—my greatest desire in writing *Unchained*.

I'd like to ask something of you, please. Consider sending a note or email and social media post to your friends and family, sharing your experience from reading *Unchained* and encouraging them to purchase the book from Amazon or my website: www.ronpost.org.

Your action can make a difference in other lives.

On my site, you'll find free weekly devotions and an email sign-up to receive notifications of new posts. I believe the devotionals will bless your life and all those who read them.

Thank you so much.

Ron